The Interface Experience
A User's Guide

Kimon Keramidas

T0345749

Published by the Bard Graduate Center: Decorative Arts, Design History, Material Culture
Distributed by the University of Chicago Press, Chicago and London

This catalogue is published in conjunction with the exhibition *The Interface Experience: Forty Years of Personal Computing* held at the Bard Graduate Center: Decorative Arts, Design History, Material Culture from April 3 through July 19, 2015.

Curator of the Exhibition
Kimon Keramidas

Focus Gallery Team
Director of the Gallery and Executive Editor, Gallery Publications:
Nina Stritzler-Levine
Head of Focus Gallery Project:
Ivan Gaskell
Chief Curator: Marianne Lamonaca
Focus Gallery Project Coordinator:
Ann Marguerite Tartsinis
Exhibition Designer: Ian Sullivan
Director of the Digital Media Lab:
Kimon Keramidas
Dean for Academic Administration and Student Affairs: Elena Pinto Simon

Catalogue Production
Managing Editor: Daniel Lee
Catalogue Design and Production:
Kate DeWitt
Manager of Rights and Reproductions:
Alexis Mucha
Illustrations: Joseph A. Cuillier III
Copy Editor: Barbara Burn
Proofreader: Christine Gever

Photographic Credits
Photographs were taken or supplied by the lending institutions, organizations, or individuals credited in the picture captions and are protected by copyright; many names are not repeated here. Individual photographers are credited below. Permission has been sought for use of all copyrighted illustrations in this volume. In several instances, despite extensive research, it has not been possible to locate the original copyright holder. Copyright owners of these works should contact the Bard Graduate Center, 18 West 86th Street, New York, NY, 10024.

Jonathan Muziker © The Museum of Modern Art/Licensed by SCALA / Art Resource, NY: Fig. 1

Bruce White: Figs. 5, 6, 12–16, 22–24; Pages 30–32, 40–42, 50–52, 62–64, 74–76

Typeface
This book is set in Bell Centennial and Bell Gothic Italic. Released in 1978, Bell Centennial was designed for AT&T by Matthew Carter with features intended specifically to make effective use of early digital typesetting technology. Carter subsequently based his 1996 design for the typeface Verdana on Bell Centennial. Verdana was designed for Microsoft and intended to be easily readable on screen.

Published by
Bard Graduate Center: Decorative Arts, Design History, Material Culture, New York

Exclusive trade distribution by the University of Chicago Press, Chicago and London

ISBN: 978-1-941-79202-5

Library of Congress Cataloging-in-Publication Data

Keramidas, Kimon.
  The interface experience : a user's guide / Kimon Keramidas.
    pages cm
  "This catalogue is published in conjunction with the exhibition The Interface Experience: Forty Years of Personal Computing held at the Bard Graduate Center: Decorative Arts, Design History, Material Culture from April 3 through July 19, 2015."
  Includes bibliographical references and index.
    ISBN 978-1-941792-02-5 (paperback)
  1. Microcomputers--History--Exhibitions.
  2. User interfaces (Computer systems)--History--Exhibitions. I. Bard Graduate Center: Decorative Arts, Design History, Material Culture. II. Title.
    QA76.17.K37 2015
    004.16--dc23
                          2014049146

Printed by GHP, West Haven, Connecticut

24 23 22 21 20 19 18 17 16 15   1 2 3 4 5

Contents

Director's Foreword

The Bard Graduate Center has been a pioneer in developing digital media in teaching, research, and exhibiting, so it is only appropriate that the ninth Focus Project should examine the developing character of users' experiences with digital tools. *The Interface Experience* takes us from the appearance of the Commodore 64 in 1982 to that of the Microsoft Kinect in 2010. Linear development alone is not what the curator of the exhibition and author of this catalogue, Kimon Keramidas, seeks to present. The experience he has in mind centers on handling working examples of five devices, each of which requires a particular set of manipulative responses on the part of the user. To emphasize the role of the user in these relationships between person and machine, we have produced the catalogue in the form of a user's guide, evoking the kind of publication that accompanied early home computers.

As the director of the BGC Digital Media Lab, Dr. Keramidas has guided students, faculty, and staff in innovative uses of new digital resources, especially in teaching. As an assistant professor on the BGC faculty, he plays a leading role in developing the academic study of those resources. In preparation for this exhibition, Dr. Keramidas offered "The Interface Design Experience Tutorial" in the fall semester, 2014. The students who participated in the tutorial, and who contributed substantively to the project, are: Emily Banas, Martina D'Amato, Caitlin Dichter, Andrew Gardner, Alana Jiwa, Jane Kilmar, and Cynthia Kok.

This project is unusual because, rather than drawing on institutional collections, Dr. Keramidas assembled all the devices included—the five that are the focus of attention and the ancillary exhibits—from the online "retro" market. He did not have to treat them as pristine objects of industrial design but was free to do with them whatever was appropriate to the project. This meant resuscitating their capacity for interactivity. The software designer Jonathan Dahan produced working programs for the five central devices, enabling visitors to live or relive the unique interface experience with each of them. Complementing this effort, CHIPS, led by Adam Squires, Dan Shields, and Teddy Blanks, produced the web application that provides information on the objects in the exhibition.

The dean of the Bard Graduate Center, Peter N. Miller, makes the Focus Project possible through his invaluable support of this collaboration between the Gallery and the Academic Program of the BGC. Complementing his attentions are those of Elena Pinto Simon, dean of Academic Administration and Student Affairs; Nina Stritzler-Levine, director of the Gallery; and Ivan Gaskell, professor and head of the Focus Gallery Project, who oversaw the project.

Staff members of the Academic Program and the Gallery collaborated to realize Dr. Keramidas's concept: Kate Dewitt, art director; Eric Edler, Gallery registrar; Alex Weiss Hills, digital designer and website manager; Marianne Lamonaca, associate Gallery director and chief curator; Daniel Lee, director of publishing; Alexis Mucha, manager of rights and reproductions; Stephen Nguyen, exhibition preparator and installation coordinator; Ian Sullivan, exhibition designer; and Ann Marguerite Tartsinis, associate curator and Focus Gallery Project coordinator. The production of this catalogue was aided by the diligent work of our copy editor, Barbara Burn, and proofreader, Christine Gever. I extend my thanks to them and to all other members of the faculty and staff of the Bard Graduate Center whose dedication has made *The Interface Experience* possible.

> —Susan Weber
> Director and Founder
> Iris Horowitz Professor in the History of the Decorative Arts
> Bard Graduate Center

Foreword

One of the avowed purposes of Kimon Keramidas's Focus Project is the
evocation of memories, specifically recollections of using various personal
computing devices. Each time someone sets out to use a new or previously unfamiliar device, she hopes to move from the challenge of the first
encounter to the eventual acquisition of easy familiarity. Although some
features of each device may create their own challenges, on balance users
hope that the specifics of their designs might serve to ease that transition. Dr. Keramidas invites us to attend to design factors in detail when
considering each of the five devices he has selected. However, he pro-
poses that acquiring that familiarity is not simply a matter of passively
conforming to predetermined skill expectations, but it is also a matter of
creative performance on the part of the user. The user of a Commodore 64
or an Apple Macintosh in the 1980s developed and sought to perfect a
performance no less than does the user of a Microsoft Kinect from 2010
onwards. Dr. Keramidas's background in theater and performance studies
informs his presentation of digital interfaces no less than does his
knowledge of the technologies involved.

The project concerns people and machines in intimate relationships, which
is why Dr. Keramidas went to such lengths to ensure that visitors to the
exhibition would be able to interact physically—and emotionally—with the
devices themselves. The evocation of memories is an integral part of the
interface experience in this exhibition. These memories vary with the age
and culture of the users, but insofar as people have used digital devices
that other, newer ones have superseded, a residue of earlier, often outmod-
ed skills remains latent in the minds and somatic capacities of those users.
I no longer recall the keyboard commands that I learned when operating
my first home computer in 1985 (an Amstrad PCW8512), but were I to
unpack and turn on that old machine, it seems possible that I would recall
at least some elements of a forgotten repertory of skills that enabled
me to perform with it.

The Interface Experience does far more than foster nostalgia, though
nostalgia can be a powerful historical tool as well as an opportunity for
self-indulgence. In this exhibition, Dr. Keramidas asks us to consider what it

is to lose and to recall skills associated with digital devices, as well as to acquire them in the first place. He invites us to ponder just what might be occurring when experiences evoke memories of forgotten routines.

—Ivan Gaskell
   Professor of Cultural History and of Museum Studies
   Curator and Head of the Focus Gallery Project
   Bard Graduate Center

Acknowledgments

In the Bard Graduate Center, Susan Weber has built a remarkable and unique institution, one that continually inspires all of its members to think in new and creative ways about the ever-present impact of material culture on human life. Dean Peter N. Miller and Gallery Director Nina Stritzler-Levine have fostered and allowed this project to thrive, and the enthusiasm and continued support from both the academic and exhibition staffs at the BGC have created a wonderful home for me and for this project.

In addition to everyone already singled out in the Director's Foreword, I'd like to thank professors David Jaffee and Catherine Whalen as well as Academic Programs staff members Jamie Cavallo, Marc LeBlanc, and Keith Condon, who have all been immensely helpful in giving shape to this project.

My family provides continuing inspiration, both intellectual and emotional. My brother, Jason, and sister-in-law, Aurelie, balance humor and geekiness equally, while my parents, Vassilis and Elaine, have given me their unconditional support. Their experiences working in science and technology have had a profound influence on my own life and work.

Most of all, I would like to thank my wife, Margaret Magnarelli, and our wonderful son, Milo. Being able to share this experience with them has been thrilling, whether discussing the finer points of the project with Margaret or watching our toddler yell at our Kinect to get our Xbox to do things.

Introduction: What's Wrong with This Object?

A few years ago, when I was visiting the Museum of Modern Art in New York City, I was happy to see that an Apple Macintosh computer was in the museum's permanent collection of design objects. Computers are a significant part of our culture, and because the specific nature of their design is an important feature that can be strongly linked to histories of design and art, they merit a place in museums. However, there was something not quite right about its presentation, something that I did not fully understand at the time. The Macintosh was behind glass, without a keyboard, not powered up, and definitely not meant to be touched (fig. 1). It was presented, as most things in a museum are, in a manner intended to provide visitors with a relatively intimate but ultimately removed and passive relationship with the objects on display.

Fig. 1. Installation view of the exhibition, "Standard Deviations: Types and Families in Contemporary Design," March 2, 2011–January 30, 2012. The Museum of Modern Art, New York.

After that first experience with the Macintosh in a museum display, my own relationship with computing technologies and museum practice changed. I began to consider how technologies such as the first Macintosh that are now so ubiquitous in our daily life fit into our material experience of the world. This caused me to reflect on that visit to MoMA and the empty feeling I had when viewing the Macintosh. What was it about my experience that had been so problematic?

1   Brenda Laurel,
Computers as Theatre
(Reading, MA: Addison-
Wesley, 1993), 10.

First, I considered the way in which computers are different from the things we typically see in a museum. For the most part, objects in an art museum like MoMA have been made to be seen, not used. Paintings, sculpture, and works on paper are all primarily visual artifacts, and they are displayed in museums so that visitors may see them. They are also often unique and priceless, and inter-action with them is therefore limited because of the potential for damage. These reasons are logical, and they extend to many design objects in museums like MoMA, where they usually serve as examples of iconic pieces, such as a World War II Jeep or a Dyson vacuum cleaner, which were designed for use but are now being maintained for the sake of preservation and display. Although these objects may still be usable, they are often static enough for us to merely imagine their use and unique enough that the museums are justified in not allowing visi-tors to touch them.

The more I thought about this issue, however, the more I realized that the computer is a different kind of object, no matter how notable its visual de-sign. Brenda Laurel writes in *Computers as Theatre* that a "computer-based representation without a human participant is like the sound of a tree falling in the proverbial uninhabited forest."[1] As such, presenting a computer but preventing the involvement of a participant (or user, in the common parlance of interface and interaction designers) really is not representative of what is important about that particular piece of culture. After all, it is not simply the hardware in isolation that made the Macintosh memorable; the introduction of the mouse in conjunction with a new graphical user interface (GUI) and software designed for that interface made it stand apart and fostered a new kind of personal computing.

Therefore, when we consider the most effective way to present a device such as the Macintosh in a museum exhibition, it is very important to understand how an interface between user, hardware, and software produces a meaningful expe-rience. "Experience" is a widely used but also somewhat vague and potentially tricky word, so let's consider how it fits into an understanding of computers as historical objects. In phenomenology—the philosophical study of the structures and properties of experience and consciousness—our lived experience is made up by the ways in which we perceive, think about, act upon, and feel about things in the world. Central to this understanding of experience in phenomen-ology is a sense of intentionality in the objects we perceive. In this context, intentionality does not refer to whether or not something is done on purpose, but rather it refers to the many ways—whether through sensory perception, thought, desire, or memory, for instance—by which an object is constituted and experienced by us.[2] Accordingly, this book and exhibition will consider the user's experience of an interface such as the Macintosh, with an eye toward the way we perceive, think about, and even desire this category of objects, particularly during those moments in which we are using them. The computers must be used, thought about, and related to as platforms for dynamic interactive experiences, for this is really what the experience of these objects is about in our daily life. Presenting them as static hunks of plastic, silicon, and metal is an incomplete and ultimately irrelevant approach to demonstrating their relative importance to human culture. And this importance is no small thing, because personal computing devices are the mass-consumed representations of a paradigmatic shift in the way information shapes our daily life.

In his seminal essay "The Computer for the 21st Century," Mark Weiser writes that "the most profound technologies are those that disappear. They weave themselves into the fabric of everyday life until they are indistinguishable from it."[3] Writing in the early 1990s, Weiser postulated that ubiquitous computing technologies would achieve such a status within the first twenty years of the twenty-first century and bring people closer together by drastically increasing our capacity to access information and to communicate with each other. Although the inability to distinguish computing experiences from everyday action can be seen as the Holy Grail from the perspective of computer interface design, it is not without potential pitfalls in the understanding of the role of computing technology in everyday life.

The decoupling of the individual from the physical experience of computing has the potential to distance the user from a tactile and conscious understanding of the role of technology in society and move him toward a less-aware and surface-level engagement with the world around him. Concerned with such a trend in contemporary society, Jean Baudrillard writes in "Xerox and Infinity" that:

> the new technologies, with their new machines, new images and interactive screens, do not alienate me. Rather, they form an integrated circuit with me. Video screens, televisions, computers and Minitels resemble nothing so much as contact lenses in that they are so many transparent prostheses, integrated into the body to the point of

2   David Woodruff Smith, *Husserl*, 2nd edition (London and New York: Routledge, 2013), 180–84.

3   Mark Weiser, "The Computer for the 21st Century," *Scientific American* 265, no. 3 (September 1991): 91.

4   Jean Baudrillard,
"Xerox and Infinity," in *The Transparency of Evil: Essays on Extreme Phenomena*, trans. James Benedict (London and New York: Verso, 1993), 51–60.

5   Viktor Shklovsky, "Art as Technique," in *Russian Formalist Criticism: Four Essays*, trans. Lee T. Lemon and Marion J. Reis (Lincoln: University of Nebraska Press, 1965), 779.

being almost part of its genetic make-up. . . . All our relationships with networks and screens, whether willed or not, are of this order. Their structure is one of subordination, not of alienation—the structure of the integrated circuit. Man or machine? Impossible to tell.[4]

Baudrillard sees the computerized individual as unable to recognize his utter reliance on technology. In order to highlight this potential for subordination and absorption into the spectacle of technological culture, it is therefore important to historicize these technological objects. Exhibition settings, through their pedagogical capacity to motivate intellectual engagement, can provide the context for that historicization. They can also provide a platform for experiences and forms of spectatorship that allow for a more objective consideration of the role of computing devices in our daily lives.

The exhibition that this book accompanies—*The Interface Experience: Forty Years of Personal Computing*—hopes to achieve these goals. It will facilitate for visitors the possibility of seeing technologies that are increasingly ubiquitous in everyday life as if for the first time. In the essay "Art as Technique," Viktor Shklovsky wrote that "after we see an object several times, we begin to recognize it. The object is in front of us and we know about it, but we do not see it—hence we cannot say anything significant about it."[5] Shklovsky believed that one could work against such a sense of familiarity with a thing by showing it from a different perspective that separated it from its normal use, whether in art or daily life. In this way an object would be separated from an automatic sense of recognition and made to stand out as different, recognizable, and able to be analyzed. This process is one that has come to be known as defamiliarization. This exhibition will use the reframing practices of defamiliarization to allow visitors to reconsider not only the historical objects on display, but also the technologies they use in their daily life, by engaging them in active and tactile experience of different interfaces. Rather than allowing visitors to passively observe objects from the past, this structure will encourage them to experience interface on a personal as well as didactic level and to recognize how those technologies play a role in shaping their own experiences and the conditions of contemporary society. In this moment of defamiliarization, the objects will become more clearly situated in a historical context that reveals not only their materiality and design, but also their role in shaping a contemporary cultural infatuation with technologies that are the newest, the best, the most revolutionary.

One of the central aims of this project is to make possible a critical aware-ness of the role that the personal computing industry plays in shaping our desires and expectations of technology. All of the devices discussed in this book and on display in the exhibition are the products of corporations whose practices are guided by the competitive forces of a capitalistic marketplace. Rather than institutions guided by pure research principles, these corpora-tions develop products that are designed to be successful in a system driven by profit and fierce competition. That market impetus leads to powerful and pervasive marketing campaigns and strategically devised rhetoric that fetishizes and valorizes these devices as prostheses vital to our existence. Likewise, a taste for the next big thing has been developed for us, along with the belief that planned obsolescence is justified. By looking to the near past and reflecting on our individual personal histories of interface experiences, we can better understand just why we carry a particular phone in our pocket or choose a certain desktop or gaming console for use at home. From this point of clarity, we can begin to establish a position from which to under-stand our relative agency in those decision-making processes, our complicity in the role of the technology industry in our society and on our environment, and find ways to escape the structure of subordination that Baudrillard warns us about.

This book is intended to serve as a companion to the exhibit by examining the terminology of the interface; providing historical reflection on objects, people, and places; and proposing ways of telling the story of personal computing in exhibition spaces. The essay "What Is Interface Experience?" discusses the complex notion of the experience of the interface. Whether interface is consid-ered to be the very real physical hardware we use, the visual metaphors pro-vided to us by software, or a more elusive and ephemeral surface of interactions between human and machine, the way in which we conceive of the experience of that interface is an important foundation for understanding personal computing technology. "Performing the Experience of Interaction" describes how these concepts and objects all come together to form an exhibition that both questions historical modes of display and shows how unique computing devices are in the history of material culture. Lastly, "Objects of Experience" considers the five objects that are the focus of the exhibition and examines how the development of their hardware, software, and experiential design allows us to ask questions about the way we use interfaces and the market forces that have led to certain developments in personal computing.

6   Manuals were jokingly used as a marker of interface usability in an early ad comparing the Macintosh, with its slim user guide, to the IBM PC and its stacks of binders. *MacIntosh Manuals*, 2012; http://www.youtube.com /watch?v=AAK3hPOLBAY&fea ture=youtube_gdata_player.

A Note on this Book's Design

The design of this book—including the wire binding, tabs, and iconographic and technical drawings—is meant to draw out interesting parallels between computing as a new medium and the old media materials that have supported and instructed us in the use of computers.[6] This book parallels that history, as it is a paper companion for an exhibition with significant digital components. To tell the visual history of those old media materials—and to reflect on their increasing obsolescence in the age of the Internet—the book typographically suggests user's guides printed for the kinds of objects displayed in the exhibition.

In addition, you will notice that objects included in the physical exhibition or the accompanying digital platform will be highlighted **in this manner** . If you wish to learn more about any of these objects, visit http://interface-experience.org.

"Interface" is a highly contested and contingent term that deserves detailed explication. Is it the hardware? The software? The visual language of a system? Two of those? None? Something completely different? There is no shortage of literature on what different thinkers believe the interface encompasses, and, as one would expect, interpretations of the term vary greatly based on the context of its use and the mission of the project within which it is deployed. In order to grapple with the contingency of the term and the tempest of competing voices eager to define its use, we will get to where we are going through those thinkers and the different ways they have come to define and discuss the term "interface." In doing so, we can glean what we might think of as encompassing an interface and also find where there may be holes or discrepancies in the understanding of the term that we might want to fix or fill.

What Is an Interface?

In this chapter, I will work toward a definition of "interface" that will provide a better framework for understanding the experience of personal computing devices by emphasizing how the design and materiality of those devices are instrumental in shaping the ephemeral phenomenon of user experience. To begin, let's consider the origin of the term outside of computer history. James Thomson, in his nineteenth-century writings on fluid dynamics, used "interface" to describe the shared boundary where two different types of fluids or a fluid and a solid meet.[7] In Thomson's work, the interface region is a space where potential actions and behavior can occur, actions that could change the nature of the fluids and their reactions to one another.[8] Another more familiar but equally useful variant of the term is to describe material sewn or fused to the unseen side of fabric to make it more rigid. Interfacing, as it is called, lacks the design and aesthetic qualities to be a fabric that one would use alone to make a garment.[9] But when the interfacing is brought into contact with another piece of fabric and attached to it through heat or sewing, the two pieces benefit from the aesthetic qualities of the outward-facing fabric and the structural characteristics of the interfacing.

These examples imply a point, space, or surface of contact across which there is potential for interaction, and the dictionary definition of "interface" bears this out: "A point where two systems, subjects, organizations, etc., meet and interact: '*the interface between accountancy and the law.*'"[10] That still leaves the definition quite broad and open to many interpretations. There is nothing wrong with that, but in order to come to a more concrete understanding of how the term relates to the experience of personal computing, we must put the term

7   James Thomson, "Continuity of States in Matter," in *Collected Papers in Physics and Engineering*, ed. Joseph Larmor and James C. Thomson (Cambridge: Cambridge University Press, 1912), 276–333; http://archive.org/details/collectedpapersi00thomrich, 327.

8   For more on fluid dynamics and the origination of the term "interface," see Branden Hookway, *Interface* (Cambridge, MA: MIT Press, 2014), 59.

9   "Interfacing," *Wikipedia, the Free Encyclopedia*, July 5, 2014; http://en.wikipedia.org/w/index.php?title=Interfacing&oldid=541144576.

10   "Interface," *Oxford Dictionaries* (Oxford: Oxford University Press); http://www.oxforddictionaries.com/us/definition/american_english/interface.

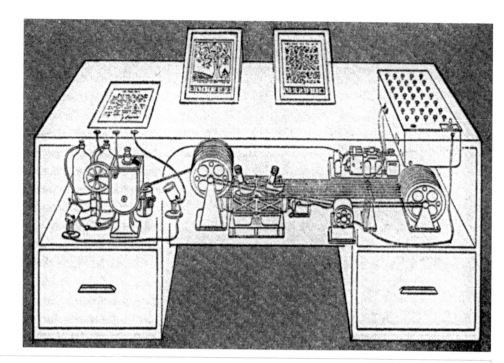

Fig. 2. Alfred D. Crimi and James Lewicki. Hypothetical memex from illustrated reprint of Vannevar Bush's "As We May Think," *Life*, September 1, 1945.

11   Vannevar Bush, "As We May Think," *Atlantic Monthly* (July 1945): 101–8.

in the context of early computer systems to show how designers and theorists perceived the point where computers and users came together.

The earliest ideas of what computer interfaces might look like and how they should behave can be seen in the work of three scientists working during the 1940s, '50s, and '60s: Vannevar Bush, Norbert Wiener, and J. C. R. Licklider. The work of these men provides insight into the thinking about computers and their use and displays the wide range of disciplines that have addressed the challenge of computer design. Bush was an engineer and inventor, Wiener a mathematician and philosopher, and Licklider a psychologist and one of the first computer scientists.

Bush's seminal 1945 essay "As We May Think" is concerned with the enhancement of the user's experience in accessing information through improved designs of data storage and retrieval systems. In his essay Bush proposed designs for the "memex," a machine with numerous inputs and outputs for more efficiently accessing and manipulating what were then analog records on microfilm (fig. 2).[11] The memex was a complicated desk that stored information and allowed for input and access through a variety of key, pen, and lever controls, as well as a document scanner. Because Bush was working in an analog world, these designs have a physical approachability that is harder to find in contemporary computers, whose components have been maximized for size and efficiency by decades of miniaturization. While one could imagine pressing the memex's keys and levers or looking at the tiny images on the microfilm, a silicon microprocessor's functionality is largely invisible. As a result, there is a more direct connection between the physical design of the memex's interface (a term that Bush does not explicitly use) and the perceived improvements in information access experienced by the user.[12]

Whereas Bush was describing the components of a specific interface, Norbert Wiener's development of the science of cybernetics considered the importance of the evolving relationship between humans and machines. Wiener was concerned about the increased presence of technology in daily life. In his 1954 essay "Men, Machines, and the World About," Wiener recalled "a great engineer who never thinks further than the construction of the gadget and never thinks of the question of the integration between the gadget and human beings in society."[13] To address these concerns, Wiener set about to better understand parallels between human and machine participants in computer communications. He noted that the computer and user are both equipped with sensory apparatuses that allow them to notice changes in the information of the world around them. Both machine and human are able to internalize those conditions and perform a response that produces new information.[14] In much of Wiener's work, human and machine are connected by the ways in which they act analogously in systems that provide feedback. The experience of computing when Wiener was writing was far slower and involved noticeable time delays between the input and output of information, and in a certain sense humans and computers were operating on a similar scale of time. In contemporary computer experience, however, machines respond instantaneously, and the sensory responses of human and machine are integrated in the moment rather than in sequence over longer periods of time. This makes Wiener's writing even more resonant today, as his work both explicates and warns about the complex physical and experiential connections shared by computers and their users.

In 1960 J. C. R. Licklider developed a theory of symbiosis between humans and computers. He believed that computers could do more than just formulate

12   Vannevar Bush, "As We May Think," illustrated reprint. *Life* (September 1945): 123.

13   Norbert Wiener, "Men, Machines, and the World About," in *The New Media Reader*, ed. Noah Wardrip-Fruin and Nick Montfort (Cambridge, MA: MIT Press, 2003), 71.

14   Norbert Wiener, *The Human Use of Human Beings: Cybernetics and Society*, Da Capo Series in Science (New York: Da Capo Press, 1988), 26–27.

15   J. C. R. Licklider, "Man-
Computer Symbiosis," in *The
New Media Reader*, 74–82.

solutions to numerical problems, and he wanted computers to be involved in the thought process required to solve more complex problems. He believed that this would be achievable by improving the interactive platforms by which humans and computers communicated and cooperated. Along with proposing the reorganization of memory and language structures in computer systems in order to better suit the two sides of the symbiotic relationship, Licklider made specific suggestions as to what types of interface equipment would be required. He wanted users to be able to interact with computers through three input technologies: desk surfaces that could be drawn and written on in a manner legible to the computer; networked wall and desk displays that would allow for a team of users to present materials to one another and to the computer; and automated speech recognition technology that would enable the user to communicate in real time with the computer without having to learn new languages or speed typing.[15]

Although the physical scale of computers at the time seems incongruous with our experience of computers today—computers in 1960 still took up entire rooms—Licklider's desire to integrate multiple physical inputs is still useful when one considers the scope that an interface can encompass. In human-computer symbiosis, the humans and the machines are equal partners in a relationship that is made possible by communication through physical devices. This system also represents the type of cybernetic relationship that Wiener outlines, as the communicative system relies on inputs and feedback responses from both human and machine. During the period in which Bush, Wiener, and Licklider were working, the materiality of the computer was more visible than it is now because of the relative scale of the computing experience. As the microprocessor and transistor had yet to exert an influence on computing technologies, this was an era of room-sized mainframes, punch cards, and vacuum tubes. But as computers became smaller, cheaper, and more accessible, greater possibilities were afforded the individual user. It was during this transition that the term "interface" began to be used more frequently as a part of computer design discourse.

The works of Bush, Wiener, and Licklider were mainly conceptual or analytical, but Douglas Engelbart's research in the 1960s was aimed at developing usable systems that would improve human intellect. Engelbart hoped to augment human intellect in four ways: through artifacts, language, methodology, and training. The artifacts represented the physical features of Engelbart's project and were "objects designed to provide for human comfort, for the manipulation of things or materials, and for the manipulation of symbols."[16] Engelbart's understanding of the "man-machine interface" was that it was a boundary or coupling across which energy flowed when human actions and artifact actions were exchanged. He believed the interface to be a border condition that occurred when the human interacted with the machine, not something that consisted of the user and/or material artifacts of the computer. In this sense, it was even less substantial than Thomson's fluid dynamic interface, which at the minimum consisted of the molecules at the intersecting points of the two liquids.

Noted design theorist and cognitive psychologist Donald Norman has frequently grappled with the materiality of the interface and the most effective way to design computer systems for human use. Norman sometimes interprets the term as a fleeting threshold, much as Engelbart did, while at other times he takes a position that focuses on the importance of the material conditions of the interface. In his essay "Cognitive Artifacts" (1991), Norman placed the interface between a person and what he called cognitive artifacts, artificial devices "designed to maintain, display, or operate upon information in order to serve a representational function."[17] The interface in this case provides an interpretable representation for the user of what the computer as cognitive artifact creates as it operates upon information. Furthermore, Norman provides a model of how "interface" operates within the relationship between a human and the computer as a type of artifact or thing, but the materiality or immateriality of the interface remains ambiguous. The distinct separation of user, interface, and artifact belies the simultaneity of three elements while one uses a computer. Norman notes that the interface has style and format, but he does not clarify whether he thinks those designed features are constituted within the representations and responses provided by software or are within the physical surface of the screen.[18]

In another essay, Norman wrote that "the real problem with the interface is that it is an interface. Interfaces get in the way. I don't want to focus my energies on an interface. I want to focus on the job. When I use my computer, it is in order to get a job done: I don't want to think of myself as using a computer, I want to think of myself as doing my job."[19] Something that is not there cannot get in the way, at least in the sense that Norman implies here. The interface has to be more than a transitional phenomenon; it has to be

16 Douglas C. Engelbart, "Augmenting Human Intellect: A Conceptual Framework," *Doug Engelbart Institute* (October 1962); http://www.dougengelbart.org/pubs/augment-3906.html.

17 Donald A. Norman, "Cognitive Artifacts," in *Designing Interaction: Psychology at the Human-Computer Interface*, ed. John Millar Carroll, Cambridge Series on Human-Computer Interaction (Cambridge: Cambridge University Press, 1991), 4: 17.

18 Ibid., 26.

19 Donald A. Norman, "Why Interfaces Don't Work," in *The Art of Human-Computer Interface Design*, ed. Brenda Laurel and S. Joy Mountford (Reading, MA: Addison-Wesley, 1990), 210.

20   Johanna Drucker, "Performative Materiality and Theoretical Approaches to Interface," *Digital Humanities Quarterly* 7, no. 1 (2013); http://www.digitalhumanities.org/dhq/vol/7/1/000143/000143.html.

21   Jef Raskin, *The Humane Interface: New Directions for Designing Interactive Systems* (Reading, MA: Addison-Wesley, 2000), 2.

something that has substance and can provide resistance. If Norman experienced the graphical user interface as a barrier, it would follow that the microprocessor limitations, monitor technology, and design of the mouse through which the GUI functions also hinder the user's experience. In this case, the obstruction Norman describes must be something that is experienced as a result of the way he has intended the computer, in a phenomenological sense, and not as a temporarily incarnated threshold.

If Engelbart's and Norman's concepts of the interface are placed at a distance from a physical, tangible experience of computing, we can see in the writing of Jef Raskin—who initiated the ▐ Macintosh ▌ project at Apple—a conception of the interface as a physically substantiated part of the computer experience. By the late 1970s and early 1980s, when Raskin started designing computers at Apple, the conditions and parameters within which interface design was happening had begun to change. Bush, Wiener, Licklider, and even Engelbart were working from a tradition of engineering that focused on pragmatic approaches to efficient information processing.[20] Furthermore, they were working in military, government, or academic settings, where the focus was more on pure research than on product development. As a result, their work addressed a computer user as part of an almost mechanistic practice. But once the Altair 8800 made its debut in 1975, a bona fide personal computer marketplace emerged, and the industry began to think not only about the development of large-scale computer mainframes accessible to only the wealthiest companies, but also about the office and home computer user, who would require a very different kind of interface experience. For this reason, designers had to start thinking about the salability of a device in ways that government and academic researchers had not. Their designs would have to take into consideration consumers making market decisions based not only on pragmatics such as specifications and capabilities, but also on emotional and personal responses to a device.

Raskin believed that the computing platforms produced prior to the Macintosh in both mainframes and personal computers did not provide nearly the level of usability that they should, and he began looking for solutions. For Raskin, "the way you accomplish tasks with a product, what you do and how it responds—that's the interface."[21] This definition recognizes that there is more to designing personal computer interfaces than particular technical and functional specifications, and that in order to create a compelling interface experience, the manner in which the computer's design enables use of that system is of the greatest importance.

What makes Raskin's work compelling, both in written form and in the Macintosh as a product, is that his approach to interface synthesizes the design of hardware, software, and user experience. This is particularly notable in a series of texts Raskin composed in 1979 that would be the first outline of the parameters for the Macintosh. In laying out general hardware specifications, Raskin defined the shape of the computer, the type of monitor and keyboard, and the suggested price. He also listed design parameters focused on more esoteric experiential principles for the device: it should not become a "tangle of wires"; there should be "no computer jargon on the key-tops"; and the machine should be learnable and easily serviceable. Raskin did likewise when discussing software criteria. Alongside the technical specifications of what programming languages should be used, Raskin emphasized that software should be consistent and intuitive.[22] Raskin was conceiving of the interface of the Macintosh even at this early stage as a totality, developing a product where the hardware and software were connected fundamentally to the goal of generating a certain kind of experience for the user. This was a philosophy that aimed at creating a computer that would, in Raskin's own words, "be truly pleasant to use, that will require the user to do nothing that will threaten his or her perverse delight in being able to say: 'I don't know the first thing about computers.'"[23]

Despite Raskin's best attempts to assert the interface as a comprehensively designed platform for experience, the development of the Macintosh has actually caused the fields of computer design, human-computer interaction, and new media studies to narrow the view of what should be considered when discussing interface. Because of the success of the Macintosh and subsequently of Microsoft Windows, the GUI, with its windows, icons, and desktop metaphor, have come to represent the idea of interface for most people. This is in part because the success of these platforms resulted in very little change in the design of computers until the recent explosion of mobile computing devices such as the PalmPilot and the iPad. The typical setup of keyboard, mouse, computer, and monitor was designed for use with these types of operating systems, and this standardization has pushed awareness of the importance of hardware in the interface experience to the background. This is visible in one of the core texts of new media studies, Lev Manovich's *The Language of New Media*.

22 Jef Raskin, "General Criteria," in *The Macintosh Project: Selected Papers from Jef Raskin (First Macintosh Designer)*, circa 1979; http://www.sul.stanford.edu/mac/primary/docs/bom/gencrit.html.

23 Jef Raskin, "Design Considerations for an Anthropophilic Computer," *Making the Macintosh: Technology and Culture in Silicon Valley*, May 29, 1979; http://www-sul.stanford.edu/mac/primary/docs/bom/anthrophilic.html.

24 Lev Manovich, *The Language of New Media* (Cambridge, MA: MIT Press, 2002), 11.

25 Ibid., 69.

26 Ibid., 115.

As a wide-ranging text that aims to catalogue and organize the various aesthetic components of new media, Manovich's book places the interface alongside operations, illusions, and forms. Whereas the other sections focus on software, appearance, and commonly used conventions within new media, the interface chapter is about the human-computer interaction (HCI) and operating system.[24] It becomes clear that for Manovich the relationship between human and computer is narrowly delineated and restrictive. In 2002, when the book was published, the experience of the Internet through the browser was challenging the dominant paradigm of the desktop-metaphor GUI. For this reason, Manovich's consideration of the interface focuses completely on the metaphorical, aesthetic, and semiotic conditions of the desktop. There is only one sentence that expands the idea of the interface beyond these considerations into the material conditions of computers as new media machines: "HCI includes physical input and output devices, such as a monitor, keyboard, and mouse."[25] Manovich's narrow view of the interface and his interest in the formalistic study of the iconography, cultural expression, and data-intensiveness of new media works lie in his connection to cinema. Manovich is making a critical move that aligns the screen experience of using a computer with the screen experience of cinema. He even describes the conditions of restrictions these different screens impose on the user/viewer: "Dynamic, real-time, and interactive, a screen is still a screen. Interactivity, simulation, and telepresence: As was the case centuries ago. We are still looking at a flat, rectangular surface, existing in the space of our body and acting as a window into another space. We still have not left the era of the screen."[26]

This construction of a media experience linked to more passive modes, such as film and television, is not limited to Manovich, as many new media critics and theorists understand the interface as consisting solely of the screen and the software viewed within that space. Approaching computers in this way focuses on a very limited portion of the history of interface design. Devices such as the PalmPilot, iPad, and Kinect have popularized different shapes for devices and expanded the variety of forms of input, moving past Manovich's accepted paradigm of monitor, keyboard, and mouse. As a result, the digital industry must now design software and web experiences to respond to a wide range of interface experiences. These developments affirm that the material design of an interface remains important in shaping both the experience of computing as well as the cultural forms Manovich highlights.

Even the critics who challenge Manovich's aesthetic and formalistic understanding of the GUI as interface seek to place increasing distance between
"interface" and the materiality of the personal computer experience. Alexander
Galloway, in *The Interface Effect* (2012), directly responds to Manovich's text,
asserting that its formalist methodology wrongly approaches computers and the
realm of new media as "essencing" machines that idealize platforms for virtually infinite possibility. Galloway is concerned that thinking of these machines in
this way extracts them from the realm of critical cultural discourse by denying
that they are in fact contingent, historical objects that play a significant role in
determining and shaping the course of cultural development.[27] Galloway's book
in many ways shares the goals of this exhibition project by placing the concept
of interface in a historical context to better situate the impact it has on our
culture. But Galloway's "interface effect" is about computing experience only
insofar as it maintains that software as a whole is inherently unworkable and
reflects the obstructions that inevitably arise in digitally mediated communication. Galloway critiques the political conditions of our digital culture, and as
such his work is more invested in unpacking the social implications of software
structures than the lived experience of the devices on which that software runs.
In fact, Galloway explicitly strips the objectness from the computer in his discussion, stating that "the computer is not an object, or a creator of objects, it is
a process or active threshold mediating between two states."[28] Galloway uses
"interface" as a broad term to highlight practices and effects that extend not
only throughout cultural production, but also across society, and he looks to use
the analog of the effect of interface to enable political and ethical interpretation
of a whole field of possible texts and conditions. His is the broadest expansion
of the term away from a sense of objectness and materiality, and as such shows
not only the complexity of the term, but also the ease with which the direct
and impactful experience of physically interacting with technology can be dis-
missed and abstracted.

Anchoring the Interface in Experience

The variety of usages of "interface" employed in the texts above is informative in that it demonstrates the level to which the term can be interpreted and
abstracted. It is notable that the point in history at which each of these texts
was written colors its usage, reaffirming the contingent nature not only of the
experience of interface, but also of theorization about and critique of that experience. Branden Hookway in *Interface* (2014) has argued that the point where the
interface happens is "neither fully human nor fully machine; rather, it separates

27 Alexander R. Galloway,
The Interface Effect
(Cambridge and Boston: Polity,
2012), 19–20.

28 Ibid., 22.

29   Hookway, *Interface*, 44.

30   Brenda Laurel,
"Introduction," in *The Art of
Human-Computer Interface
Design*, xii.

human and machine while defining the terms of their encounter."[29] In this definition, the interface is explicitly not a thing, but a relationship that manifests itself only when human and machine interact. This approach provides a platform from which to question positivist approaches to technological development and its implications for humanity. But by claiming that the interface exists solely as an intangible relationship between computer and user, Hookway deemphasizes the very tangible lived experience of personal computing. In abstracting the interface in this way, Hookway has taken the teeth out of his own argument for the importance of the interface. Like many of the texts discussed above, the assertion that the human and machine exist apart is meant to enable a questioning of how technology augments the human. This separation reduces the interface to an intellectual construct.

We know, however, that the give-and-take between user and computer happens not just as a practice of discourse. Brenda Laurel provides a corrective to this decoupling when she writes that "an interface is a contact surface. It reflects the physical properties of the interactors, the functions to be performed, and the balance of power and control."[30] Laurel's definition reminds us that the interface is a tangible foundation of the computer experience. If the interface is a contact surface, then it can be argued that it is the place where the physical interaction between the user and the computer is materially constituted. The user's experience of this place is not just in how one engages with or intends the surface, but in the whole of the machine as the user expresses himself through the keyboard, mouse, stylus, finger, or sensor, cognizant that the computer will recognize the input and respond with feedback. The interface as materially constituted is therefore the result of the physical conjoining of both human and machine, consisting in toto and simultaneously of the brain as thought producer, the body as action executor, the input device as interaction receiver, the processor as input translator, the software as feedback generator, and the screen as feedback provider. Understanding the interface as this connection of parts situates the computer experience in a tangible reality, rather than at the level of pure discursive analytics. Theorizing the objectness out of the interface, as Hookway and others have done, ultimately denies the importance of the material in understanding the symbiotic, cybernetic, and augmentative characteristics of the computing devices that play such a central role in our cultural life.

Reasserting the materiality of the interface in this way is not just an exercise in defining parameters for the use of the term. It is also meant to emphasize a direction from which we can approach computers and their history within a broader cultural context. The near ubiquity of computing devices in our lived experience raises serious questions about how these technologies influence everyday life in both visible and invisible ways. Baudrillard warned that, as we increasingly rely on computers to manage our lives without understanding how, the ubiquity of these devices can cause a subordination to the structure of the integrated circuit. To avoid this, we must perceive the interface experiences not just as an individual interaction with a computer, but also within the context of larger sociocultural and technological systems. This means that the computer objects featured in this book and exhibition are addressed from a perspective that includes their design, manufacturing, distribution, reception, perception, and use. This strategy helps us to better understand the artifact and system within society.[31] From keyboards to mice to styluses to touchscreens, the material design of computers has shaped how they respond to our actions and how we respond to their feedback. As such, the design of hardware becomes central to our understanding of the experience of interface, because of how it determines the real and perceived affordances[32] made available to the user, both with regard to the physical interaction with the device and the range of possible operations that can be enacted via software.

Having established the material conditions of the interface, it is important to emphasize that the experience of interface is continuous, variable, and ephemeral. Erkki Huhtamo has written that "an interactive system is characterized by a real-time relationship between the human and the system. . . . In an interactive system the role of the human agent is not restricted to control and occasional intervention. Rather, the system requires the actions of the user, repeatedly and rapidly. . . . Thus an interactive system is not based on waiting, but on constant (re)-acting."[33]

To understand the interface is therefore to understand our experience of computers, while maintaining an awareness of duration and ephemerality, and to comprehend how our actions and reactions and the corresponding actions and reactions of the computer change the nature of the interface. It is through this sense of time-based lived experience that we can situate the interface experience within a historical, cultural, and social context to better understand how computers shape our lives and the world around us. As Sherry Turkle has noted, "computational objects, poised between the world of the animate and inanimate, are experienced as both part of the self and of the external world."[34] In order

31 W. D. Kingery, "Technological Systems and Some Implications with Regard to Continuity and Change," in *History from Things: Essays on Material Culture*, ed. Steven D. Lubar and W. D. Kingery (Washington, DC: Smithsonian Institution Press, 1993), 217–18.

32 The term "affordances" was introduced to design by Donald Norman, who describes real affordances as all those things that can be done with an object. Perceived affordances are those that are made perceptible and meaningful to the user through the object's design. Norman's example is the computer screen. All screens afford the ability to be touched, but only some respond to touch. The use of graphic elements to denote where to touch makes those affordances perceivable. Donald A. Norman, "Affordances and Design," *jnd.org*; http://www.jnd.org/dn.mss/affordances_and.html.

33 Erkki Huhtamo, "From Cybernation to Interaction: A Contribution to an Archaeology of Interactivity," in *The Digital Dialectic: New Essays on New Media*, ed. Peter Lunenfeld, Leonardo Series (Cambridge, MA: MIT Press, 1999), 106–7.

34 Sherry Turkle, *The Second Self: Computers and the Human Spirit*, 20th anniversary ed. (Cambridge, MA: MIT Press, 2005), 5.

to understand an interface in an exhibition or as an object of study, we must therefore be able to ascertain what kind of personal relationship we can build with that device. We must consider how that relationship changes over time as we use it and determine from real and perceived affordances how our conception of that device influences our understanding of our larger relationship with computational culture.

The impulse behind this exhibition and book is to highlight the changing experience of interfaces in personal computing technology. The goal is to resituate these computing interfaces, which are usually forgotten once they become obsolete, so that people can be more critically aware of computers in a world where they are becoming increasingly invisible and ubiquitous. Exhibitions offer a unique platform for such an exploration because they provide a useful pedagogic framework in which to consider an object removed from potentially confusing contextual conditions.

For instance, computers in a home or workplace are so entwined in larger networks of behavior and actions and have become so commonplace that they can easily be taken for granted. The exhibition removes these devices from that environment and makes it possible for museumgoers to ponder their history and operations, not as nostalgic relics of their own experiences but as markers of different stages in the development of personal computing. That being said, what makes most exhibitions valuable pedagogically also tends to prevent interaction with the objects, which in the case of this particular group is crucial to fully understanding them. As the introduction to this book affirms, traditional display models are untenable if the exhibition is not itself interactive and does not incorporate both hardware and software elements. Without these, the display of a Macintosh computer, like the one at MoMA, is not a representative experience.

The challenge is to constitute an experience for the museumgoer that takes advantage of the pedagogical possibilities of the exhibition but also takes into account the interactive nature of these objects as interfaces. One way to address this challenge is to think of the parallels between exhibition, interface, and performance space. Brenda Laurel equates the experience of interactivity with that of performance, writing that "the material cause of a human-computer activity, and also of a play, is the enactment—that which unfolds before a person's senses. As plays employ the sights and sounds produced by actors moving about in scenic environments, computers may employ graphics, sound and music, text characters, and even tactile and kinesthetic effects."[35] "Performance," like interface, is a multi-variant and context-dependent term.[36] Laurel's use of the word is deliberately straightforward in connecting performance and theater, as her project seeks to create parallels between interface design strategies and Aristotle's *Poetics*. When she writes about performance, she refers specifically to actors "performing" actions on a stage. My use of

35   Laurel, *Computers as Theatre*, 10.

36   One particularly good investigation into the broad range of interpretations of "perform" or "performance" is Jon McKenzie, *Perform or Else: From Discipline to Performance* (London and New York: Routledge, 2001).

37 Laurel, *Computers as Theatre*, 10.

the term will be the same in this discussion, as I address the components of a traditional sense of performance—actors, stages, and tactile and kinesthetic effects—in the context of this particular exhibition.

Laurel's example helps set the parameters for us to consider the interface, like a stage, as a space that affords both the potential for a dynamic experience and the opportunity for the individual to effect change in that space. Laurel adds that interfaces are representational and highly context-dependent,[37] characteristics that can also be applied to exhibitions, which provide a similar kind of material experience in a physical space where visitors negotiate and interpret objects that are placed in specific contexts. All three—the stage, the interface, and the exhibition—are dynamic, live experiences in which the human presence provides a valuable variable input to established material frameworks that are designed to enable possibility, whether that possibility is drama, computing, or cultural learning.

The three experiences are, of course, differentiated by the nature of the medium within which they are experienced. As has been noted, museum exhibitions traditionally discourage interactivity, and the same can be said of the traditional staging of plays. Personal computing devices, however, require interactivity. How can one reconcile those differences in an approach that looks to engage and utilize the knowledge frameworks of all three? The exhibition's display of objects directly engages with this difference by (a) utilizing the role of participants as spectators or witnesses as an integral part of the pedagogical framework of the exhibition, and (b) integrating the interpretive texts of the exhibition within the objects, thereby allowing the experience of, discourse about, and presence of the object to exist simultaneously. To do this, the exhibition incorporates specific parameters for the spatial experience of the interfaces with both performance strategies like those used on a theatrical stage and existing methods for framing knowledge in exhibitions.

Since the objects on display are intended to evoke the personal experience of computers, the exhibition begins with a display that tells the history of changing interface design, materials, and technologies. To accomplish this, we have included working original hardware that visitors will be able to touch and use. This tactile mode allows one to feel the responsiveness of a **Commodore 64** keyboard, the contour of a Macintosh mouse, the heft of a PalmPilot, and the shape of the iPad's body. Interacting with the devices or watching someone manipulate them is a crucial part of explaining what made these particular devices important, what makes them different from one another, and how they relate to contemporary and future technologies.

When computer technologies are displayed in museums, they are usually operated through an emulator,[38] a type of software that is intended to replicate the experience of using old interfaces but not on the original hardware. The recent Smithsonian American Art Museum exhibition *The Art of Video Games* used emulation in this way in order to run vintage games on contemporary hardware. Although the use of newer hardware increases reliability, the speed and experience of the system are almost certainly skewed and the level of accuracy reduced in its portrayal of the computing experience as a whole. Because *The Interface Experience* is an experiential rather than a formal or aesthetic presentation, it requires an accuracy that emulators cannot provide.

Unlike other displays devoted to the evolution of the computer, this exhibition underscores the place of the user in the interface experience. If we consider these computer interfaces as responsive parts of a lived experience rather than as static objects, they must be presented in a way that the user's experience can be both enacted and perceived. Geographer Yi-Fu Tuan writes that "an object or place achieves concrete reality when our experience of it is total, that is, through all the senses as well as with the active and reflective mind."[39] Because this exhibition aspires to that kind of total experience, it provides both active and reflective possibilities in the staging of user interactions with the computing devices. By staging the interfaces in a way that demonstrates the computing experience to both the user and the viewer of the device's performance, each computing object is presented as something to be performed (active) and something to watch being performed (reflective).

My strategy for staging the interface experience as a dual-layered performance is based on the work of German theater director and theorist Bertolt Brecht. Brecht believed that, through the deployment of certain techniques and styles, theater could be didactic, instructive, and revelatory for the audience. He conceived of an epic theater that integrated music, text, staging, and acting style in a way that shed light upon the human condition of the spectator and aroused him or her to action against social injustice or oppression. In this epic theater, Brecht directed his actors to perform in a way that did not allow the audience to experience an intimate reckoning with characters on stage. Whereas a traditional actor

38   From *Wikipedia*: "An emulator is hardware or software or both that duplicates (or emulates) the functions of one computer system (the guest) in another computer system (the host), different from the first one, so that the emulated behavior closely resembles the behavior of the real system (the guest)."

39   Yi-Fu Tuan, *Space and Place: The Perspective of Experience* (Minneapolis: University of Minnesota Press, 1977), 16.

40   Bertolt Brecht, "The Modern Theatre Is the Epic Theatre," in *Brecht on Theatre: The Development of an Aesthetic* (London: Methuen, 1964), 33–42.

41   Laurel, *Computers as Theatre*, 10.

42   Tuan, *Space and Place*, 16.

would try to fully inhabit a character and express his or her emotions, an actor performing in Brecht's style would present the character to the audience as if wearing a mask—what Brecht called *gestus*—presenting to the audience the fiction of the character through an intentional distancing. Rather than immerse the audience in the reality of the drama, the space between actor and audience created by this style of acting compels members of the audience to defamiliarize themselves with the actions on stage. The audience can then take an alienated and more critical stance toward the ills of society being portrayed rather than responding sympathetically and emotionally to the actors. Brecht believed that this critical stance would allow theater to be more instructive and that audience members would more readily take lessons learned from the stage and feel empowered to change their own conditions and the conditions of society.[40]

Brecht's methods may be adapted to the exhibition of personal computing devices so that each active interface can act as a stage for defamilarized performance and instructive theater. As Laurel has noted, one of the most important functions of interfaces is that they generate a representation of what is going on inside the computer, making it possible for the user to perform functions on it.[41] The interfaces let us see and impact the operations that are going on at a microscopic level in the monitor and processing units of the system. As such, the representative experience of the interface is separate from but connected to reality in a manner similar to the experience presented by a performer practicing Brecht's techniques. A historic computing device that can be interacted with thus creates the potential for a defamiliarizing experience—which is the goal of this exhibition—such that the visitor enacts the performance as an actor/agent for other visitors in the space.

However, the performance alone does not enable the critical defamiliarizing experience. The exhibition space is also important here, just as the scenery and music of the theater are what set the stage in Brecht's epic theater. Because an exhibition space is an environment that is inherently didactic, people enter prepared to see objects out of context, out of place, and out of time. Tuan notes that within museums and other places of memory and conservation "the effort to evoke a sense of place and of the past is often deliberate and conscious. To the extent that the effort is conscious, it is the mind at work, and the mind—if allowed its imperial sway—will annul the past by making it present knowledge."[42] Tuan sees this annulment as a loss, but this exhibition will attempt to exploit the conflation between past and present experience in order to create the kind of experiential differences that enable defamiliarization in Brecht's theater.

The logic behind this process is as follows. If the passive display of objects in exhibitions creates an illusory past, which is in fact an incognito representation of the present, performance and interaction with objects provide an alternative experience by allowing the museumgoer to view the performance of a functioning object. This is contingent on a central factor—the design of the experience to be had by the user of the personal computing device. The interaction must be such that the practice of using the device creates a specific and unfamiliar experience for both the user and for any possible onlookers. The material nature of the personal computer as an object worthy of museum display provides an entry point and stable platform for the defamiliarizing act. The software, however, is contingent enough to be used more flexibly, and custom applications can be designed to establish and then counter the authenticity implied in an exhibition setting in a manner that mirrors epic theater.

This has been achieved here by the creation of custom software with embedded interpretive material—and coded to run on the original operating systems of each device previously mentioned—which will create the effect of a technical *gestus* being generated by the computer. Through this *gestus*, the exhibition highlights which technical affordances make each specific device historically significant. However, the software experience will not attempt to present an authentic re-creation of what it was like to use these devices in their heyday; that is simply not possible. Rather, what is highlighted are the characteristics of each device that continue to make it an important historic object in the present, especially in relation to the contemporary interface experiences that visitors will be encouraged to reflect upon. This simultaneous perception of and distancing from the past is necessary for critical introspection and defamiliarization.

In order to accomplish this sense of contemporary experience and historic reflection, the custom software is engineered to focus on use scenarios that highlight how hardware and software worked together in each object to create distinct experiences. For instance, when using the Commodore 64, visitors will have to load a program with a now unfamiliar string of numbers, letters, and symbols. They will also have to work with the stiff keyboard and use function keys that were integral to performing actions in the 1980s but are rarely used now. In the case of the Macintosh, the software experience highlights the new iconic experience of the GUI and mouse by leading the visitor through a series of icon clicks and having him or her draw and shade bitmap shapes. Presenting the opportunity to experience these physical, temporal, and modal specificities opens up the possibility of the recognition of difference and enables the defamiliarization of any individual object or the complete range of devices in concert.

It is important to restate that this defamiliarization is not meant to occur solely for the museumgoer who is participating in the constructed semi-performance via the device. The act in which that museumgoer uses that device is itself to be presented as a performance that can be watched, examined, and considered with critical distance. Although the user of the device may have an instructive defamiliarizing experience, it is equally if not more likely for observing visitors to enter a space of defamiliarization that allows them to reconsider the relevance of these massively popular objects and reflect on their own use of personal computing technologies. Thus, the spectator of the performed interaction, like the audience in Brecht's theater, is experiencing a performance that is not like reality but is intentionally structured against the grain of the "real" experience of these devices in their historical context. The physical objects may persist as relics of certain historical moments; but the software, the dynamic part of the staged experience, provides an instructive experience outside the illusion of historical reconstruction. The intention is for the spectator, who is watching the user of the interface interact with the defamiliarized device, to see both the technical *gestus* of the computer and the performance of the user as alienating strategies. This provides a visitor with a greater potential for a defamiliarized understanding of these objects and their place in personal and social histories.

The choices made in arranging the devices to accomplish the goal of staged interface were not as explicit or as obvious as those made in placing a Brechtian actor on a proscenium stage. That would be too radical a departure from traditional museum practice, and such a presentation would become the focus of the display, distracting from the experience of the interfaces. The challenge was to find a subtle staging that situated the core objects within an informative context relative to interpretive text and the other devices on display, but one that allowed exhibition visitors to watch each other interact with those devices. The solution in the end was to keep them in proximity to other devices that were relevant either because of chronology or similar affordances, but at the same time to allow them to exist as distinct islands within the small space (fig. 3). This layout created space around the devices for both the user of an interface and spectators of that user, while providing ample lines of sight for viewing the experience of interface from a distance.

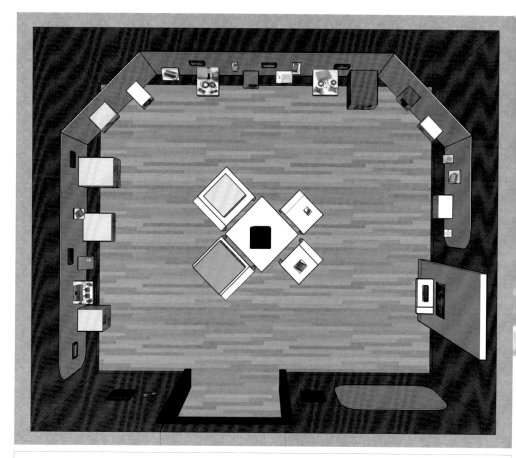

Fig. 3. Ian Sullivan. Exhibition design layout for *The Interface Experience*, 2014. Bard Graduate Center Gallery.

13   Thomas Streeter, *The Net Effect: Romanticism, Capitalism, and the Internet*, Critical Cultural Communication (New York: New York University Press, 2011), 69–92.

Experience, Defamiliarization, and Self-Reflection

This exhibition is designed as an intervention to counteract the thoughtless lived experience we have of these devices in daily life. Our interactions with computing technologies should not be considered simple and neutral, but rather as part of a complex interaction of market forces, ideological positioning, corporate rhetoric, material interaction, and representational immersion. The evolution of the personal computer has come at a particularly charged time in the political-economic life of the Western world, and the technological developments discussed so far are notable for having affected that charged sensibility as much as they have been influenced by it.

As Thomas Streeter has noted, the early days of the personal computing era coincided with broader social changes in capitalist production philosophies and consumer practices. Whereas consumer products before the Information Age were characterized by their mass-produced uniformity, personal computing is a field in constant flux and development, and it is, of course, very personal. The dynamic complexity of these devices makes acquiring them a different experience from buying a Coke or a pair of Levi's jeans, and in that sense it represents a new kind of capitalist acquisition that requires a deeper investment in understanding the device before purchasing it. Furthermore, a mythology of the genius hacker giving birth to new inventions has worked in concert with the promotion of individual entrepreneurship, a prominent narrative in the era of neoliberalism or late capitalism that has defined the last forty years.[13] The centrality of the individual in this narrative has made it easier to relate to dominant corporate entities, because they have iconic leaders, such as Apple co-founder Steve Jobs, Microsoft co-founder Bill Gates, and Google co-founders Sergey Brin and Larry Page, who are held up and heralded as relatable figures. This is one of the reasons so many computer users develop such devout brand loyalty to companies such as Apple or Microsoft and platforms such as iOS and Android. There is investment in and attachment to these devices, as well as a sense that they give us cultural capital because they are connected to the aspects of our personality in which we take pride.

Because these devices are so personal, it is often difficult to maintain a critical distance from them without being prompted by some external influence; the goal of the defamiliarizing and performative frames of this exhibition is to provide just that sort of influence. But the inflection of that influence is a difficult and complex concern. Criticism and praise of personal computing devices and their history are complicated and multivalent, as a variety of different perspectives tend to weigh heavily on the discourse surrounding the interface experience. For instance, the GUI is a frequent target for invective as an invention that ultimately has limited our understanding of computers. Author Neal Stephenson in *In the Beginning . . . Was the Command Line* attacks the desktop GUI, claiming that it uses bad metaphors to oversimplify tasks that should be valued for their complexity.[44] Apple in particular is often excoriated for foreclosing the possibilities of computing by popularizing the metaphorical desktop and discouraging access to the command line and physical innards of computing devices. Lori Emerson attacks both the desktop and mobile experiences Apple provides when she claims that the "user-friendly" Macintosh environment precludes the use of computers for creativity and learning[45] and that the iPad is "unquestionably made for consumption."[46] On the other side of this debate, the many accomplished industrial and human interface designers referred to in this text, such as Larry Tesler, Bill Atkinson, and Jonathan Ive, have spent their careers developing hardware, software, and operating systems that they believe enhance the experience of using personal computing devices. Books such as Brenda Laurel and S. Joy Mountford's *Art of Human-Computer Interface Design* (1990) and Bill Moggridge's *Designing Interactions* (2007) are testaments to the fact that although the narrative of the genius inventor may be an exaggeration, designers of the personal computer have thought long and hard about the implications of their inventions and deserve some praise for the profound impact their work has had on how we use computers and interact with the world.

The goal of this project, however, is not to pick one side of the debate on the value of specific and general developments in the interface experience and assert that position in the presentation of the materials. Rather, it is to provide a narrative of the contested ground that exists, so that visitors to the exhibition can make their own decisions as to how these devices fit into their lives and think about the relative importance that personal computers have had for society as a whole. The experience of the interface is a personal one, and intertwined in that experience are not only personal histories and a varying level of familiarity with devices, but also individual perspectives on various relevant political, ideological, and economic viewpoints. We must carefully weigh the role that the voices of the innovators and developers play in this exhibition, because their investment in the impact and legacy of these devices is influenced both by the passion they have for their creations and by the financial success and prestige those creations have brought them. Furthermore, we must keep in mind

44   Neal Stephenson, "In the Beginning . . . Was the Command Line," 1999; http://pauillac.inria.fr/~weis/info/commandline.html.

45   Lori Emerson, *Reading Writing Interfaces: From the Digital to the Bookbound*, Electronic Mediations 44 (Minneapolis: University of Minnesota Press, 2014), 84–85.

46   Ibid., 19.

how most of these innovators worked within corporate frameworks that remain focused more on profit and competition than on philanthropic advancements in the realm of human capability, which is what interested pure researchers such as Engelbart and Alan Kay. Market forces are very powerful in the business of personal computing, especially in the realm of hardware, where high production costs mandated by material production rely on a capitalist structure of sales, profit, and investment.

For these many reasons, the exhibition structure of *The Interface Experience* is a complex model that seeks to create a tight integration of rhetoric, performance, interface, and experience. This approach is necessary because the personal nature of computing objects makes their presentation in a traditional exhibition incongruous with the experience of their use in an everyday context. The challenges that the complexity of these objects present in exhibition practice are representative of the paradigm shifts that personal computing has caused across society and throughout our culture. The forty years under consideration have seen significant changes in the economic and technological forces that drive society, with the forces of capitalism and the market both impacting and being impacted upon by the political and social conditions of a world driven by computers. As we analyze and critique the role that interfaces play in our daily lives, it remains important that we do so from a position of historical understanding and intellectual distance. One can easily imagine, as interface design evolves at an ever-quickening rate, that we could lose our grasp of where we have come from as we contemplate the endless and dizzying possibilities of where we are headed. Sometimes, in order to regain our bearings, we must break with the familiar and everyday, and perform the experience of interaction.

Although the history of the personal computer covers only the past forty years, the number of different computers, mobile devices, and specialized interfaces, such as game consoles, that make up that history feels almost incalculable. Driven by a ferocious and hyper-competitive market predicated on new features, lower prices, and market share, computer companies are always creating new models with new capabilities. The challenge of this project has therefore been to navigate through that history and choose a focused set of interfaces that best represent how personal computing has found its way into our lives.

Certain specific factors have determined the process for selecting these objects, which resulted in a group of five examples. First of all, the interfaces that are the central points of the exhibition are those that best represent the total lived experience of the interface. Each interface is significant not for its individual hardware or software or operating capabilities, but rather for the way in which the object as a designed product combined those three into a highly functional experience that left its mark on the history of computers. Secondly, these devices each represent a significant landmark in physical design that materially changed our experience of computing. Whether that change is in the form factor of computing to make it possible in the home—changes in input devices from the keyboard to mouse to finger, or changes in scale to enhance portability or usability—each device represents a significant stage in an ever-changing material relationship between humans and computing devices. Lastly, each object is notable for its political and economic impact on the field of computing. All five of these objects have sold millions of units, and as such their ubiquity and durability in the marketplace have rendered them symbolic of different eras in the development of personal computing.

Based on those parameters, five devices stand out as representative of significant stages in the development of personal computing:

> Commodore 64
> Apple Macintosh
> PalmPilot
> Apple iPad
> Microsoft Kinect

In the following five essays, I will discuss how each of these devices created a specific interface experience. Each tells a unique story about design processes, product development, market reception, and user application and describes how each device has shaped our culture through its dynamic materiality.

The Commodore 64—
Embodying a Revolution

```
**** COMMODORE 64 BASIC V2 *
 64K RAM SYSTEM  38911 BASIC BY
READY.
```

In 1983, for the first time, *Time* magazine named a non-human as person of the year, declaring the personal computer the "Machine of the Year" (fig. 4). It was a justified selection, as the previous eight years had seen the personal computer firmly established as an important part of everyday life. In 1975 Ed Roberts started Micro Instrumentation and Telemetry Systems (MITS) and released the Altair 8800, which is widely recognized as the first personal computer. Although the Altair, with an unwelcoming interface, never really made it past the purview of enthusiasts ravenous for computing power in their homes, its modest commercial success motivated other entrepreneurs to experiment with the possibilities of personal computing.

47   "Most Important Companies," *Byte* (September 1995).

Fig. 4. "The Computer, Machine of the Year" from *Time*, January 3, 1983, fold-out cover. © 1983 Time Inc.

In 1977, a little more than a year after the Altair's release, three personal computers, which were later dubbed the "1977 Trinity" by *Byte* magazine, made their way to the marketplace: the Commodore PET (Personal Electronic Transactor), the Apple II, and the Tandy–Radio Shack 80 (TRS-80).[47] These computers provided a second generation of interface experience that was much more accessible than the Altair and embodied all that was exciting and frustrating about the personal computer revolution.

48   The development of the spreadsheet software VisiCalc or the Apple II is particularly noteworthy, as it kept that platform afloat. Apple had been struggling to sell units in 1978 and 1979. Fortunately for the company, the author of VisiCalc wrote the program on an Apple II he had borrowed, and as a result it came out first for that computer. Business computing users quickly saw the value of VisiCalc and soon equated the Apple II with the software, helping sales of the computer to spike upon its release in late 1979. For many people, VisiCalc and its capabilities alone justified the purchase of a personal computer, thereby making it the first killer app.

49   Steven Weyhrich, *Sophistication & Simplicity: The Life and Times of the Apple II Computer* (Winnipeg, MB: Variant Press, 2013), 55.

50   Steven Stengel, "Commodore PET 2001 Computer," *Obsolete Technology Website*, December 10, 2013; http://oldcomputers.net /pet2001.html.

51   Stan Veit, "The Commodore 64," *PC History. org*; http://www.pc-history .org/comm.htm.

On the positive side, each computer was more accessible than any previous personal computer, providing programming capability as well as the ability to run prepackaged software. The software capabilities were particularly important, because these computers were able to perform operations beyond mere calculation, including basic word-processing tasks, games, and eventually spreadsheet management.[48]

On the negative side, the monitors were often unsightly, and only the Apple II could produce color. Sound was also limited. Using the computer was often difficult as well, with programs loaded from external sources by noisy, slow, and often finicky cassette tapes that were eventually replaced by disk drives.[49] Input was usually cumbersome, with clunky keyboards necessitating strings of arcane commands. The original PET keyboard was particularly troublesome, as Commodore, which had originally been a calculator company, used a calculator-style keyboard with tiny Chiclet buttons that precluded touch-typing.[50] These computers also faced production problems; Commodore dealers found that as many as four out of every ten computers they sold would need to be repaired or replaced.[51] The TRS-80 was unfortunate enough to earn the moniker "Trash-80," as a result of its unreliability.

Despite these flaws, these three computers opened up the possibility that a much larger audience would be able to own personal computers. Before the

Fig. 5. Commodore 64 with 1702 monitor and 1541 disk drive, 1982.

Fig. 6. Top and rear views of the Commodore 64, 1982.

Altair in 1975, there was no home computer market, and even by 1977 fewer than 50,000 personal computers had been sold. By 1980, however, thanks in large part to the market parameters set by these three models, about one million personal computers had been sold, and the personal computer revolution was well on its way.[52] Within the early stages of this revolution, the Commodore 64 (fig. 5) is in many ways representative of the type of experience and kind of machine with which people were interacting. Originally released in August 1982, just a few months before *Time*'s famous computer issue, the 64 would go on to sell about 12.5 million units between 1982 and 1994, making it the best-selling computer of all time.[53]

The 64 was the direct successor to the VIC-20, the company's second major product after the PET. The 64's visual lineage from the VIC-20 was unmistakable. Both devices were single-piece units that looked like an overweight keyboard and shared the same boxy design aesthetic, with rounded edges developed by the designer Nishimura in Commodore's Japanese offices (fig. 6).[54] The only thing that distinguished the two on the outside was the color of plastic: the 64 was a darker shade of beige.[55] Like the VIC-20, the 64 unit housed the motherboard, random-access memory (RAM), and an impressive array of connections for external data sources and peripherals. No monitor, disk drive, or cassette deck was included, but the 64 could easily plug into a television and could run software on cartridges that were plugged directly into the back of the unit. Commodore made a concerted effort to make the 64 affordable by setting its initial price at $595. This price point was more affordable than contemporaneous computers such as the IBM PC 5150, which was released in 1981 for $1,565, and the Apple IIe, an update to the Apple II, released a few months after the 64 for $1,395.[56]

52   Jeremy Reimer, "Total Share: 30 Years of Personal Computer Market Share Figures," *Ars Technica*, December 15, 2005; http://arstechnica.com/features/2005/12/total-share/.

53   The actual number of Commodore 64s sold is an oft-debated topic. Commodore's founder, Jack Tramiel, has claimed that the company sold between 22 and 30 million units, although others have calculated that the number is closer to 17 million (Reimer). A recent detailed analysis of sales reports has tabulated that number to be 12.5 million units (Steil), a number that seems to be most rigorously supported and likely to have been true. Computer History, *Commodore 64—25th Anniversary Celebration*, 2007; http://www.youtube.com/watch?v=NBvbsPNBIyk&feature=youtube_gdata_player; Jeremy Reimer, "Total Share: Personal Computer Market Share 1975–2010," *Jeremy's Blog*, December 7, 2012;

http://jeremyreimer.com
/m-item.lsp?i=137; Michael
Steil, "How Many Commodore
64 Computers Were Really
Sold?," *Pagetable.com: Some
Assembly Required*, February
1, 2011; http://www
.pagetable.com/?p=547.

54   Brian Bagnall,
*Commodore: A Company
on the Edge* (Winnipeg, MB:
Variant Press, 2010), 263.

55   The Commodore 64's
body came to be known af-
fectionately as "the breadbox,"
but it was also derisively called
"the doorstop." Benj Edwards,
"Inside the Commodore 64,"
PCWorld, November 4, 2008;
http://www.pcworld.com
/article/152528/comm64.html.

56   Steven Stengel, "IBM
5150 Personal Computer,"
Obsolete Technology Website,
December 10, 2013;
http://oldcomputers.net
/ibm5150.html.

57   "iMac Intel 27" EMC 2639
Teardown," *iFixit*; https://
www.ifixit.com/Teardown
/iMac+Intel+27-Inch+EMC
+2639+Teardown/17828.

58   Interestingly, both Apple
and Commodore were relying
on the same company, Shugart,
for their disk-drive heads. In
the end, however, Wozniak was
able to design a faster drive
and deliver it to market sooner
with the same parts. Bagnall,
Commodore, 169–71.

One particularly notable feature of the 64's design was how custom hardware was involved in creating such a product in the early days of the personal computer market. Computers today are for the most part assemblages of off-the-shelf components created by a variety of companies. For instance, iMacs made in the past few years have a processor and controller made by Intel, a display made by LG, and a graphics card made by NVIDIA.[57] There is still invention and innovation at a per-part level, but many computers are alternate assemblages of similar sets of components. In the early days of personal computer design, however, one thing that often distinguished competitors was the ability to design new hardware technologies that would improve the quality, speed, and performance of these new machines. For instance, the efficient disk drive that Steve Wozniak designed for the Apple II was a market differentiator, beating Commodore to the punch in its quest to design a drive for the PET.[58]

One of Commodore's greatest advantages in this regard was its ability to design microprocessors, the chips that do all of the calculation in a computer, for the specific needs of their computers. Key to this was Commodore's acquisition of the semiconductor chip company MOS Technology in 1976. Having MOS as part of the company enabled Commodore to experiment and innovate with new chips, starting with the central processor of the PET 6502, which had been designed by Chuck Peddle, a microchip engineer who would lead Commodore's computer projects during the PET years. This chip, which MOS Technology developed under the guidance of Peddle before the Commodore acquisition, provided Commodore with a low-cost alternative to competing chips from Intel and Motorola and enabled the company to emerge from the calculator business and develop its own computer division.

The value of having a chip-manufacturing division within Commodore was apparent in the difference in technical capabilities as the company progressed from the VIC-20 to the 64. Although the chassis and keyboard of the VIC-20 and the 64 were virtually identical—the early prototypes of the 64 were in fact called the VIC-40—the insides were quite different. Despite its somewhat ungainly appearance and lack of included peripherals, the technical specifications of the 64 were impressive. The 64's VIC-II graphics chip was a modification of the 6502 architecture that had initially been developed as a chip for a video game console. This chip, designed by Commodore engineer Al Charpentier, provided the 64 with a rich set of visual capabilities that made it appealing to the burgeoning game development market and set it apart from most other home computers at the time. Just as significant was the sound interface device (SID) audio chip that engineer Bob Yannes designed for the 64. The SID chip provided a range of possibilities for audio that would remain unparalleled for years to come, and it remains an important milestone in the development of computer audio capabilities. Lastly, in order to coordinate all of the advanced processing done throughout the 64, Commodore engineers also designed a special logic chip, the programmable logic array (PLA), to manage the usage of the computer's memory. Together, these three chips gave the Commodore 64 a remarkable audio-visual experience for its time and price point, which is one reason why so many games were developed for the platform.[59]

The most significant technical feature, however, was undeniably the 64 kilobytes of RAM at such an affordable price. At the time of its release, no other computer offered 64K of RAM standard, and those that could expand to 64K or near to it could not compete in price. This amount of available memory meant that the Commodore quickly could run complicated programs easily, a challenge of memory that continues to this day. The 64K of RAM was so important to the identity and marketing of the computer that it became part of the product's name. As far as physical experience goes, the keyboard, while functional, was listed as one of the top ten worst keyboards of all time by *PC World*.[60] Perhaps the worst offense was the ergonomic challenge that the height of the chassis created (fig. 7). Because the keyboard was elevated an inch or two higher than keyboards

59   Ibid., 369–82.

60   Benj Edwards, "The 10 Worst PC Keyboards of All Time," *PC World* (November 1, 2007); http://www.pcworld .com/article/139100/the _10_worst_pc_keyboards _of_all_time.html.

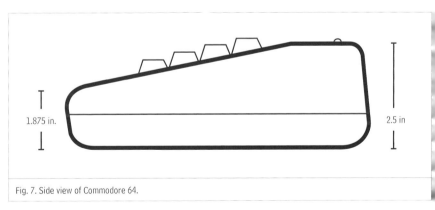

Fig. 7. Side view of Commodore 64.

we are accustomed to today, the shape of the 64 caused wrist discomfort after prolonged use. There was no good way to rest one's forearms and reach the keyboard. The keys on the 64 were clunky, noisy, and stiff—an experience that was not uncommon for computers of this era, particularly at this price point.

Fig. 8. Top view of Commodore 64 keyboard with Run/Stop and Commodore button indicated with arrows.

61   Lori Emerson has noted that this was a problem on many computers of the time, the result of a lack of standardization of interface across the industry. Commodore had its special keys in special locations, as did Apple and Radio Shack. Responses to this incongruity can be seen in computer publications of the time. For instance, *Byte* magazine ran a two-part series by Chris Rutkowski that laid out what he called the Human Applications Standard Computer Interface (HASCI), which was an attempt to standardize interfaces as a way to make computers easier to use. Emerson, *Reading Writing Interfaces*, 77; Chris Rutkowski, "An Introduction to the Human Applications Standard Computer Interface, Part 1: Theory and Principles," *Byte* (October 1982): 291–310.

Also, the layout was unusual, with keys such as Run/Stop and a special Commodore key added to the standard QWERTY format (fig. 8).[61] There were graphical icons that were helpful for programming, but they made the keyboard visually confusing to a beginner. Nevertheless, the keyboard layout was recognizable enough to an audience whose previous experience with information input was most likely on a typewriter, and that, combined with the scale and shape of the unit, made it familiar and less intimidating than a larger single-unit computer.

Along with its relatively banal exterior design, the 64 was not the most technologically advanced of the early personal computers; the Apple II series with its more complex features and hardware expandability could probably be given that title. Nor was the 64 the one that had the most wide-reaching impact; the IBM PC and its hordes of clones that would come to dominate the market for decades can likely claim that. Nor was it the least expensive; computers such as the **Sinclair ZX-81** sold at the same time for far less. What it did do, however, was create a synergy of design, features, cost, and experience that in the aggregate represent, more than almost any other machine, what it was like to use a personal computer in the late 1970s and through much of the 1980s. Perhaps most importantly, it is the computer that, thanks to its sales and Commodore's marketing strategy,[62] brought the interface experience into the homes of Americans, where people were able to explore the entertainment, productivity, and creative possibilities of computing that until recently had been stashed away in university, military, and corporate facilities.

In the *Time* "Machine of the Year" issue, Roger Rosenblatt wrote that "this sweetheart here, this little baby, looks like any ordinary machine, isn't that so? A mess of screws and buttons, a whole heap of plastic. Comes with new words too: RAMs [random-access memory] and ROMs [read-only memory]. Think that's what the machine is made of, do you—the hardware and the software and the mouse? Not a chance. The computer is made of you, lady. It's got you all inside it."[63] This sentiment—that the computer would allow a user to manifest her own individuality and have meaningful experiences with it—explains why computers of this era captivated so many people. The Commodore 64 was affordable; its software library of more than 10,000 titles made it expansive;[64] its programmability made it customizable; and its popularity made it comfortable and easy to use. The Commodore 64 really was a computer for the masses, and the continued affinity shown for it thirty years later by amateur programmers and gamers reveals how powerfully it was able to embody the thrill of experiences with early personal computer interfaces.

62   Commodore's founder, Jack Tramiel, was famous for coining the slogan "We like to sell to the masses, not the classes." *Jack Tramiel "Computers for the Masses Not the Classes" (Δεκέμβριος, 1995)*, 2012; https://www.youtube.com/watch?v=G7rUWVfS01M&feature=youtube_gdata_player.

63   Roger Rosenblatt, "A New World Dawns," *Time*, January 3, 1983; http://content.time.com/time/magazine/article/0,9171,953631,00.html.

64   ComputerHistory, *Commodore 64—25th Anniversary Celebration*, 2007.

The Apple Macintosh— The Mouse and GUI Enter the Scene

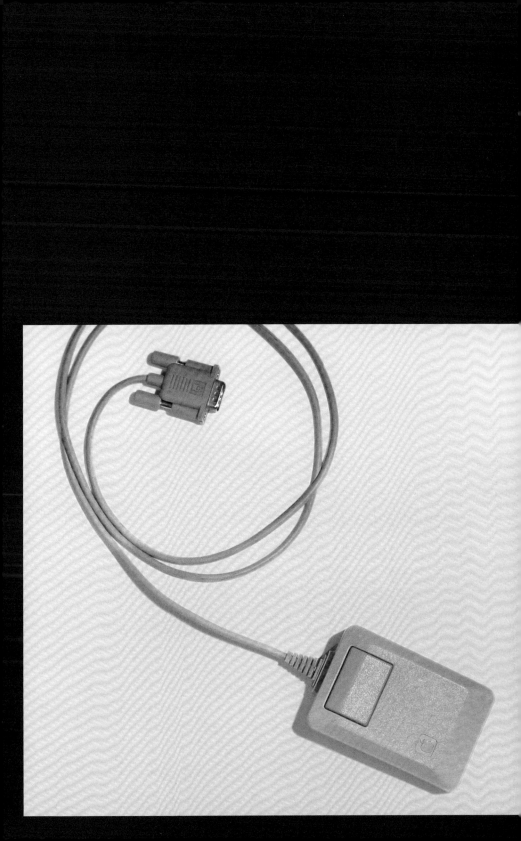

If the Commodore 64 was notable for being representative of an era of personal computing, then Apple's Macintosh is historically notable for making a very specific change in the way most of us experience interfaces. These days we take GUIs—with their windows, icons, menus, and pointers (WIMP)—like those of Windows' and Apple's operating systems for granted. But before the introduction of the Macintosh, this accessible and highly visual (rather than textual) approach to computing was unknown to most computer users. And when the Macintosh introduced the GUI, it did so with a flourish for which Apple has come to be known. There are not many computers that are embedded in collective cultural memory because of their advertising campaigns as much as they are for their technologies, but the Macintosh was a different type of personal computer. As such it changed not only the way we experience interfaces, but also the way we come to identify with and contextualize those experiences in our broader cultural life.

Perhaps the most disappointing thing about the Macintosh approach to interface experience is that it took so long to come to fruition. As early as 1962, Douglas Engelbart—whose ideas on augmenting human intellect have been discussed above—was working with his research group at Stanford University on a system based on a mouse and windows that would presage much of what would come to the market in the Macintosh. Engelbart famously showed the progress his group had made in a presentation that has come to be known as "the mother of all demos." In it, Engelbart demonstrated a system devised in conjunction with furniture manufacturer Herman Miller that included a keyboard, one of the first mice, and a five-button interface that allowed for chorded input, much like a piano (fig. 9). Engelbart used the three different inputs together in order

Fig. 9. Douglas Engelbart, William English (first mouse prototype). NLS (oN-Line System) interface designed by Engelbart's group in conjunction with Herman Miller, 1968. SRI International.

65   SRI International, *1968 Demo—FJCC Conference Presentation Reel #1*, 1968; http://archive.org/details /XD300—23_68HighlightsARes earchCntAugHumanIntellect.

66   Paul E. Ceruzzi, *A History of Modern Computing* (Cambridge, MA: MIT Press, 2003), 260–61.

67   Description of the creation of the Alto can be found in Michael A. Hiltzik, *Dealers of Lightning: Xerox PARC and the Dawn of the Computer Age* (New York: HarperBusiness, 1999), 69–77.

to move the pointer across the screen, activate different images, texts, and hyperlinks, and display the use of windows within a graphical layout.[65]

Engelbart's design was clearly a huge step forward in the realm of user input. The mouse in particular was a superior method of interacting with a computer system, because it took advantage of hand-eye coordination, a skill that humans had developed through evolution and that was much more embedded in cognitive practice than the relatively young keyboard.[66] Despite the obvious improvements that Engelbart's system provided, it received little recognition and was not adopted by computer makers at the time. Nevertheless, it did influence the development of research on input devices at Xerox's soon-to-be-established research facility, the Palo Alto Research Center (PARC).

Xerox PARC was established in 1970 in response to Xerox's concerns over what the "paperless office" would do to its copying business. One of the most significant technologies to come out of Xerox PARC was the **Alto**. This was the first computer designed with a bitmapped screen (each pixel could be given a value and represent more complex graphics than simpler displays of early personal computers) and GUI with a desktop metaphor to ease the user's interpretation of the computer's functions. In addition, the Alto was driven by SmallTalk, a programming language that made it easier and faster to design functions that in previous languages would take complex and complicated commands, and it could be connected to other Altos to allow for network communication.[67] Many of the Alto's innovative functions would come to be important features in the success of the Macintosh and the GUI. Nevertheless, it would take a number of years for Apple and other companies to find a way to make these new technologies marketable.

Although the Macintosh is almost always considered the brainchild of Steve Jobs, a number of designers and engineers contributed to the product's development. Many of them were involved in the project before Jobs was, and were instrumental in developing the design, look, and feel of the computer. Larry Tesler, who worked on the Alto and SmallTalk projects at PARC, and Bill Atkinson worked together to develop the GUI. Burrell Smith designed the innovative internal circuitry that allowed the Macintosh to perform complex computations, despite the fact that the physical container of the machine was so compact. Susan Kare designed the icons and fonts used on the computer and gave the Macintosh much of its aesthetic look (fig. 10). Before all these contributors, however, came Jef Raskin. In the discussion above of interface experience, I referred to Raskin's

Fig. 10. Susan Kare. Five icons designed for the orignal Macintosh, 1983.

theories and approaches in a general fashion and made a specific reference to the Macintosh project. It was, in fact, Raskin who started the Macintosh project at Apple with a small group in 1979. Their goal was to create a low-cost computer that was easy to use and offered a range of applications that would appeal to the average user.[68] Steve Jobs did not begin to pay close attention to the project until it was well under way in early 1981. After winning a power struggle that saw Raskin leave the company, Jobs changed the parameters of the project, aspiring to create a more expensive computer with a bigger feature set and the now-famous vertical form factor.

In the end, one of the most important contributions that Raskin made to the Macintosh project was to arrange two trips to Xerox PARC so that Apple engineers and executives could watch the Alto work. The second trip is often cited as the moment when Jobs brilliantly and completely stole the idea for the Macintosh from Xerox. But in reality Raskin and his team had been working on many of the principles of the Macintosh, including a bitmapped screen and the integration of new types of pointing devices, long before those visits.[69] It was, however, during that second trip that Jobs became enthusiastically enamored with Alto's hardware and software design, stating: "I remember within ten minutes of seeing the graphical user interface stuff, just knowing that every computer would work this way some day. It was so obvious."[70] Upon returning to Apple, Jobs mandated that the mouse would play a significant role in shaping the interface experience of the Macintosh, something that Raskin did not agree with at the time.

The Macintosh was the first successful mass-market computer to include a mouse as an input device along with the keyboard. Two previous computers had been released with mice, notably the **Xerox Star** (the commercial descendant of the Alto) in 1981 and Apple's own Lisa in 1983, but both of those were commercial failures due to poor marketing, lack of compatible software, and high costs, and as such neither can be considered to have raised public awareness of the mouse in quite the same way as the Macintosh did. It was with the release

68   Raskin, "General Criteria."

69   Alex Soojung-Kim Pang, "The Xerox PARC Visit," *Making the Macintosh: Technology and Culture in Silicon Valley*; http://www-sul.stanford.edu/mac/parc.html.

70   Hiltzik, *Dealers of Lightning*, 342.

71 The on-and-off-again relationship between Apple and Chiat/Day, specifically between Steve Jobs and creative director Jim Clow, has had a profound impact on Apple's advertising. Along with "1984," Chiat/Day created ads for the Apple II, the 1997 "Think Different" ad campaign, and the 2003 "I'm a Mac" campaign that pitted Windows against Macs.

72 jupiter2, "Apple Advertising and Brochure Gallery 3," *The Mothership*; http://www.macmothership.com/gallery/gallery3.html.

73 *Steve Jobs Introduces the Original Macintosh—Apple Shareholder Event (1984)*, 2013; http://www.youtube.com/watch?v=YShLWK9n2Sk&feature=youtube_gdata_player.

of the Macintosh that Apple began to show a marketing acumen and advertising savvy that continues to this day and is still rarely matched. Apple has long been aware of the value of selling a lifestyle fostered by their products' particular interface experiences.

With the Macintosh, Apple fully embraced the possibilities of a profound marketing campaign, as the company looked to draw attention to the Mac, with its mouse and innovative GUI, as a superior and more accessible alternative to its computing predecessors. Three events show how Apple wholeheartedly deployed this approach to marketing. The first was the showing of the now famous "1984" commercial during Super Bowl XVIII. This sixty-second film, directed by Ridley Scott of *Alien* and *Blade Runner*, was an audacious advertising move that pitted the Macintosh against the IBM PC and its clones without actually mentioning the computer or showing any pictures of it (fig. 11). It remains to this day one of the most important advertisements ever to air and is one of the many notable ads produced for Apple by the renowned marketing firm Chiat/Day.[71]

Fig. 11. Chiat/Day. Still from Macintosh "1984" television commercial, 1983.

The second marketing event was a twenty-page spread in the January issue of *Newsweek* introducing the Macintosh, the GUI, mouse, printer, and software, and the now-famous tagline "Introducing Macintosh. For the Rest of Us."[72] The third was a presentation of the computer to Apple shareholders, one of the earliest examples of Jobs's presentational panache.[73] These three events helped elevate the mystique of the Mac as they sacralized the computer, touting its revolutionary and welcoming capabilities. They played an important part in shaping the identity of the Macintosh as more than just a machine. The Mac marketing campaign attempted to change perceptions of the personal computer from an inaccessible technical object to an enabler of a creative, accessible lifestyle to which everyone could aspire.

Although the marketing campaign and design of the Macintosh helped it achieve iconic status for having changed personal computing,[74] the first version of the Mac to be released was notable more for promise than for actual performance. The advanced new operating system took up almost all of the available 128 kilobytes of RAM, which meant that running applications was a painfully slow process. Furthermore, the inability to load programs easily into memory required lots of tedious swapping in and out of different floppy disks to make the computer run. Interestingly, this is a perfect example of the challenge involved in creating innovative user experiences at the cutting edge of personal computing. Whereas the design was extremely enabling, and the software and operating system were easy to use and visually logical, the material foundation for all of that to run on—the hardware—was underpowered. As a result, the whole interface experience of the Macintosh 128K, as it has come to be known, was tangled, ponderous, and frustrating.[75]

The quality of the hardware of the first Macintosh would eventually impact its salability, and the brisk sales to early adopters within the first few months of launch came to a grinding halt around Christmastime in 1984. Fortunately, many of the problems of the original Macintosh—low memory, the drain of the complex operating system on that memory, limited expandability, a shortened keyboard without keypad, function, or cursor keys—would be ameliorated over time. In 1985 Apple released a Macintosh with 512K that could finally run more complex programs, and in 1986 most of these problems were resolved with the release of the **Macintosh Plus** (fig. 12).

74   Leander Kahney provides a fabulous look into the life of Apple's most dedicated users in *The Cult of Mac* (San Francisco: No Starch Press, 2004).

75   Steven Levy, *Insanely Great: The Life and Times of Macintosh, the Computer That Changed Everything* (New York: Penguin Books, 2000), 185–89.

Fig. 12. Apple. Macintosh Plus with external disk drive, 1986.

76   My choice of the Macintosh Plus over the 128K version was determined by the ease by which new applications for it could be created through the HyperCard program.

77   Levy, *Insanely Great*, 217–23.

78   Jeremy Reimer, "Total Share: 30 Years of Personal Computer Market Share Figures," *Ars Technica*, December 15, 2005; http://arstechnica.com /features/2005 /12/total-share/.

The Macintosh Plus's most important improvement was its one megabyte of memory, which allowed more programs to be loaded simultaneously and greatly reduced the need to constantly swap disks in and out of the computer. In addition, the Mac Plus included an expanded keyboard and ports for expansion and the connection of peripherals (such as the much-needed secondary disk drive), finally providing the combination of innovative software, thoughtful design, and comfortable user experience for which Raskin, Jobs, and the many people involved in the Macintosh project had been aiming.[76] The Macintosh Plus would go on to be the Mac with the longest production life, lasting almost five years. Branding it as the Mac Plus ED also helped Apple make significant inroads in education markets. One important feature of the Plus was the ability to run **Aldus Pagemaker**, the Macintosh's "killer app," which made graphic layout and publishing design easy and intuitive and firmly entrenched Macintoshes as the computing choice for artistic professionals.[77]

There are two different ways to think about the impact of the early Macintosh computers. From one perspective, they can be thought of as a commercial failure. Once the IBM PC and its various clones gained traction in the marketplace, Apple was never really able to gain a substantial share of the market for personal computers. Only for a brief spell between 1991 and 1993 did the Macintosh enjoy more than 10 percent of market share, and for most of the past thirty years it has been below 5 percent.[78] This was owing in part to the hardware deficiencies of the earliest models, which slowed the cultural integration of the mouse-based GUI. Just as significant, however, was the business model of Microsoft. Bill Gates smartly recognized the value in developing Windows as the standard operating system for the burgeoning PC market. Once Windows became the norm, Microsoft gained a virtual monopoly on the computing industry.

From another perspective, it can easily be argued that the success of Windows was built upon the willingness of Apple and Jobs to develop innovative, user-friendly alternatives to the cumbersome personal computers of the late 1970s and early 1980s. Although the groundwork was laid in Douglas Engelbart's research and the work done at Xerox PARC, someone had to put that technology into the hands of consumers. Having seen work done at PARC in the 1970s, Bill Gates and Microsoft had also come to realize the value of the mouse-based interface experience, and they experimented with systems similar to those Macintosh would pioneer. It took six years, however, for Microsoft to create a version of Windows (version 3.0) that would be commercially successful and could compete with the experience offered by the Macintosh operating system. Although still inferior to the Macintosh OS in some eyes, Windows 3.0 would go on to sell 23 million units and help establish Windows as the dominant operating system in both home and office computers.[79]

In the end, the story of the GUI and interface experience comes down to different business models. Apple has always kept the development of its operating system closely linked to the development of its machines, maintaining a strong hold on the link between the software and specific hardware. Microsoft's business, on the other hand, was to license its operating system to companies that would then provide a wide range of hardware with different circuitry, input devices, and peripherals that was beyond Microsoft's control. This story has come to define the experience of personal computers ever since the release of the original Macintosh in 1984 and Microsoft's 3.1 version of Windows in 1990. It subsequently led to a competitive relationship not just between the two companies,[80] which is visible in their marketing campaigns, but also between users who identify themselves as fans of either PCs or Macs.

One particularly notable trend that has resulted from this now decades-old rivalry between Apple and Microsoft has been the willingness of consumers to form strong allegiances not only to the technologies but also to the corporations that make those technologies. The ongoing PC versus Mac debate shines a focused light on the penetration of these companies' corporate identities into our experience of these devices. In this way, the interface experience exists within a cultural context that extends beyond the computer and to the user's exposure to marketing and ads such as the "I'm a Mac" campaign, which pit a bedraggled PC persona against an idealized Mac persona. This heightened sense of corporate identity has resulted in the development of passionate fan bases for Apple, Microsoft, and now Google. This fandom reveals how personal and intimate the relationship with these devices can be and how the design of these objects can evoke a truly emotional response.

79   Levy, *Insanely Great*, 278–79.

80   Apple sued Microsoft in 1988, claiming that Windows 1.0 was full of ideas stolen from the Macintosh. Apple lost the suit on the grounds that the desktop metaphor and GUI could not be patented. It was also difficult for Apple to claim originality with Xerox's Alto and Star in existence. "Apple Computer, Inc. v. Microsoft Corp.," *Wikipedia, the Free Encyclopedia*, August 13, 2014; http://en.wikipedia.org/w/index.php?title=Apple_Computer,_Inc._v._Microsoft_Corp.&oldid=613954034; Andy Hertzfeld, *Revolution in the Valley: The Insanely Great Story of How the Mac Was Made* (Beijing and Sebastopol, CA: O'Reilly Media, 2004), 190–92.

The PalmPilot—
Making the Personal
Truly Portable

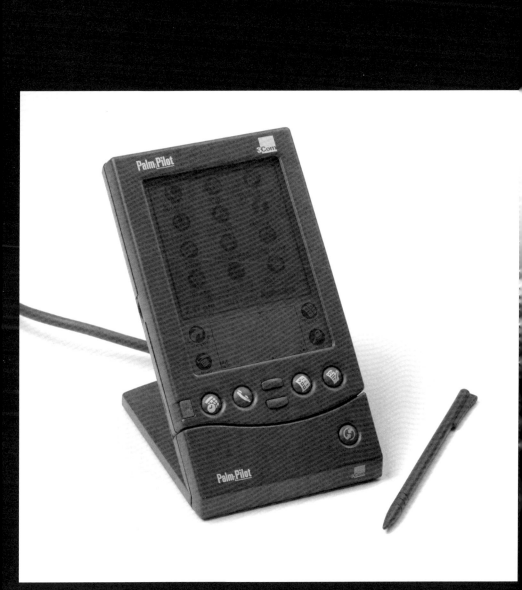

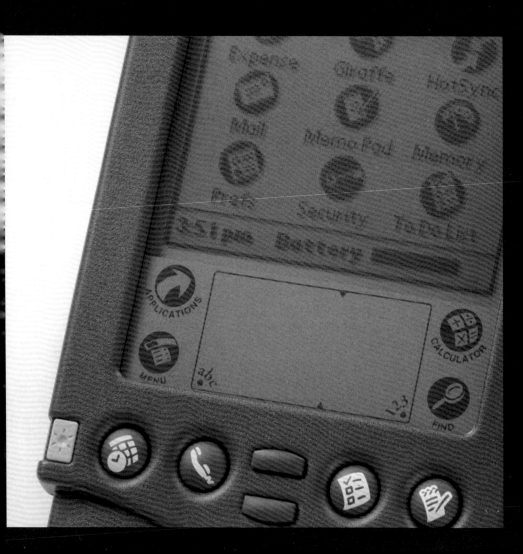

Once the usability and commercial viability of the GUI became apparent, our general sense of what it meant to use a personal computer solidified. Microsoft, through Windows, quickly spread the GUI to virtually every computer in the world, and to this day the way we interact with a computer at a desk or on a lap has stayed pretty much the same. But the personal computer category as it came to be defined in the late 1970s and early 1980s by computers such as the Commodore 64 and Macintosh does not fully encompass what it now means to use a computer in one's personal life. It would take a while, but once the desktop was well established, the miniaturization and optimization of the technologies that drive these computers was directed to new ways of making computing more portable and as a result more personal. Soon a new breed of products would move from pipe dreams and prototypes to viable and successful devices.

81   Bill Moggridge, *Designing Interactions* (Cambridge, MA: MIT Press, 2007), 162–64.

One early attempt at making computers more portable was the `Osborne 1` (fig. 13). This was a modest commercial success, but at approximately twenty-five pounds not including its battery pack, the Osborne is better known for having ushered in the brief era of "luggable" computers rather than creating a viable portable experience.[81]

Fig. 13. Osborne computer in open (left) and closed (right) configurations, 1981.

The "luggables" were followed by laptop computers, the first of which was arguably the `GRiD Compass`. Designed by Bill Moggridge for GRiD Systems, the Compass (fig. 14) was launched in 1982 and cost more than $8,000. At this price point, the computer was aimed at a business and military market, and the design mandate was to create a computer with the power of a Xerox Alto but in a durable enclosure the size of a briefcase. The process of designing the

Fig. 14. GRiD Compass 1109, 1983.

82   Ibid., 169–78.

Compass revealed the very real problems of making computers more portable, and through their solutions the GRiD team established parameters for laptop design that persist today: monitor hinging to protect the keyboard; a lightweight but durable outer shell for protection; scaling of keys and keyboard layout within a small physical footprint; and a tolerable weight for transportation. The Compass made durable portability a reality, and it was reliable and functional enough not just to remain a commercial success for a decade, but also to make it onto Air Force One and into space.[82]

The jump to true portability of the personal computing experience, however, was not to come with packaging PC- and Mac-like computers in durable cases. Luggables and laptops still ran like traditional personal computers and were designed to provide an equivalent experience. Soon companies and researchers began to imagine devices that would fit in one's pocket and respond more rapidly to a user's need for calculation, information recording and retrieval, or even game play. It was at this stage that computing had become more personal and portable, and to make breakthroughs at this scale required a dramatic rethinking of not only the device's physical parameters but also its operating system and software. First of all, these devices were imagined as much smaller and more portable than a luggable or a laptop—approximately the size of a small paper notepad or slightly larger than a man's wallet. They needed to have long battery life so a user would not have to constantly spend time charging or replacing batteries. And lastly, since they would be used on the go, they would have to start up almost instantaneously, receive data input in a way that differed from the desktop keyboard and mouse, and have quick, efficient software that would not require a lot of loading and waiting. We take these features for granted in contemporary computing, especially with the increasing ubiquity of smartphones. But in the 1980s and into the 1990s these were problems that had yet to be solved at internal hardware, software, or interface design levels.

At one point, it seemed as if Apple would quickly take hold of the market for this new category of devices with its Newton platform. The Newton was developed at Apple starting in the late 1980s after Steve Jobs had been forced out in 1985 because of flagging Macintosh sales. In search of a new market and to continue Apple's record of innovation, CEO John Sculley pushed for the development of a new handheld device he dubbed the Personal Digital Assistant, or PDA. The original Newton device, the **MessagePad** (fig. 15), first released in 1993, was approximately the size of a folded sheet of letter-sized paper and almost an inch thick.[83] Although it was not pocket-sized, the Newton was considerably smaller than desktop or portable computers, and it provided a new mobile computing experience. Information was input into the Newton with a stylus, and the device had a notepad, calendar, calculator, and other small applications. In addition, a custom microprocessor was designed by Apple to accommodate the requirements of this new category of device.[84]

Fig. 15. Apple. Newton MessagePad 120, the fourth iteration of the Newton line, 1996.

83   Steven Stengel, "Apple Newton," *Obsolete Technology Website*, December 10, 2013; http://oldcomputers.net /apple-newton.html.

84   Julie Kuehl and John Martellaro, "John Sculley: The Truth about Me, Apple, and Steve Jobs, Part 2," *Mac Observer*, January 13, 2012; http://www.macobserver.com /tmo/article/john_sculley _the_full_transcript_part2/.

85   Arun Rao, "Early Failures: Good Ideas Which Arrive Early Are Bad Products (1980–94)," Excerpts from *A History of Silicon Valley*, by Arun Rao and Piero Scaruffi, 2010; http://www.scaruffi.com /svhistory/sv/chap90.html.

86   Kuehl and Martellaro, "John Sculley."

87   Andrea Butter and David Pogue, *Piloting Palm: The Inside Story of Palm, Handspring, and the Birth of the Billion-Dollar Handheld Industry* (Hoboken, NJ: Wiley, 2002), 8.

88   Ibid., 12.

89   Ibid., 55.

The most important feature of the Newton was to be its handwriting recognition software. Handwriting recognition had been theorized as far back as Bush and Licklider, and it had been incorporated into some early stylus-based PCs, such as the Linus Write-Top. But no one had been able to make it really work. Sculley's team worked hard to get the software working reliably for the launch, but when the Newton finally went on the market in 1993, the handwriting recognition software was not ready for the demands of regular use and the device was soon struggling in sales and damaging Apple's public image. Over the next five years, Apple would spend close to $100 million on the project with only marginal sales success. Although the company was able to improve the handwriting software, the combination of over-hyping the device, the slow software, and grandiose goals eventually doomed the project, and Apple soon lost the PDA market to competitors.[85] After returning to the company in 1997, Steve Jobs killed the Newton project, and John Sculley, who himself had been forced out of Apple shortly after the Newton's initial launch, would come to regret having imagined a project that was fifteen years ahead of its time.[86]

Amid the many incremental advances that were being made in the realm of portable personal devices in the early to mid-1990s, a small group was working on its own ideas for a personal digital assistant. This group was led by Jeff Hawkins, who had previously led the successful GRiDPad project at GRiD Systems (see the next entry on the iPad for more information on the GRiDPad). But the GRiDPad, with a retail price of more than $2,500 prompted Hawkins to turn his attention to making portable devices that regular consumers—not just wealthy corporations—could afford.[87]

Hawkins's initial foray into handheld devices was a collaboration with Tandy and Casio on a project called the Zoomer. Hawkins was well aware of the change that was becoming more evident in the field of personal computing: "It's inevitable that all computing will be mobile. . . . There are so many colliding things that say, 'small, cheap, robust, on-your-person is better than big, slow, clunky, on-your desk.'"[88] Despite the fact that the Zoomer project ultimately resulted in a mediocre product—it was slow, inconveniently sized, had handwriting recognition problems like the Newton, and was expensive— it did give Hawkins the impetus to create Palm Computing to provide software for the project.[89] Learning from the mistakes of the Zoomer, Palm would refine its handheld design strategy and ultimately develop some of the most successful pre-smartphone handheld devices.

If any single object represents how to meet the challenge of designing an interface with a comprehensive understanding of the experience of that interface, it is the PalmPilot (fig. 16). Jeff Hawkins and his team were determined to simultaneously solve problems of portability, speed, and non-traditional input at a time when the industry seemed ill prepared to provide solutions. The Pilot was successful despite limited available technology and the past failures of other companies.

The first important lesson that Hawkins learned was that the technology of the mid-1990s did not enable handhelds to fully replace the desktop computing experience. What people wanted was an accessory that allowed them to carry some but not all of their information with them.[90] The second realization he made was

90   Ibid., 57.

Fig. 16. PalmPilot Professional with stylus, 1997.

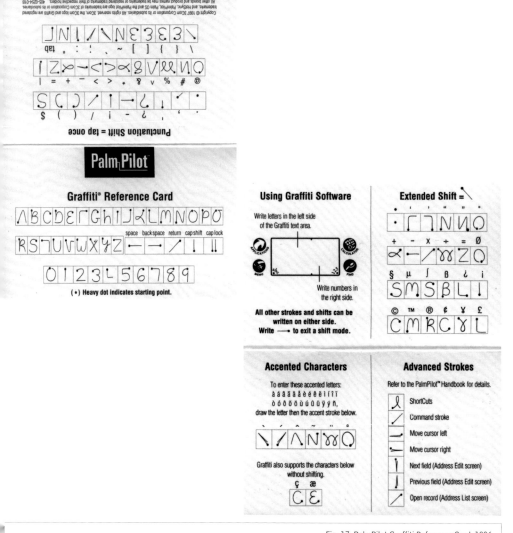

Fig. 17. PalmPilot Graffiti Reference Card, 1996.

that handwriting recognition software just was not going to work. Instead of training the computer to read handwriting, Hawkins believed he could train users to input text into a device in a better way. To accomplish this, Hawkins came up with Graffiti, a short-hand alphabet that made it easy to input text without complicated handwriting recognition (fig. 17). The software to run Graffiti was originally developed by Palm engineers Joe Sipher and Ron Marianetti for the Zoomer and Newton. However, since both devices struggled, it was not until

The Interface Experience—A User's Guide

the release of the PalmPilot that Graffiti caught on. Because Graffiti solved the text input problem without having to resort to a cumbersome mobile keyboard or relying on inaccurate handwriting recognition software, it was largely responsible for the PalmPilot's early success.

91 Ibid., 73.

92 Ibid., 73–75.

Once Hawkins established Palm Computing and freed himself from Tandy and Casio, he began developing his own platform. Convinced that the stylus could act as a foundation for handheld experience, Hawkins set four essential goals for the development of his new product: (1) Price: $299; (2) Size: Fits in a shirt pocket (fig. 18); (3) Simplicity: Fast and as easy for an average consumer to use as a Filofax paper organizer; and (4) Synchronization with the PC, since the device would be an accessory to rather than a replacement for the PC. In retrospect these goals seem relatively straightforward, as they have become the formula for designing successful devices for our mobile computing culture. But at the time, given the available technology, achieving these aims was a challenge. Hawkins had to make some radical decisions, but in the end his choices made the Palm handhelds successful.[91]

In order to ensure longer battery life, Palm's first device used an older, less energy-demanding microprocessor. Although the use of an older processor flies in the face of conventional wisdom in the computing industry, coupling that chip with a new operating system designed by Palm to be snappy while optimizing energy usage would allow the device to run for a very long time on widely available AAA batteries. Then Hawkins chose a small and relatively low-resolution screen of 160 x 160 pixels. Having a limited screen was a risk, but as Hawkins made this decision, he kept in mind the integration of hardware and software and made sure that a full day's schedule of events could be shown on a single screen. Lastly, Hawkins gambled that Graffiti would work and omitted a physical keyboard.[92]

Together with his team of engineers and designers, Hawkins worked on creating a device that would meet his challenging technological goals, while providing a responsive, accessible experience through an efficient, well-planned operating system and extended software packages. Detailed work was involved in creating physical mockups of the device, and Hawkins spent much of his day with a wooden prototype he had crafted in his pocket, intermittently pulling it out and simulating the experience of using the device. His interface designer, Rob Haitani, worked to cram all the information necessary into the tiny screen and by experimenting with

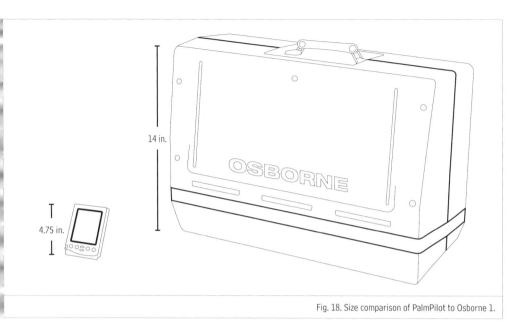

14 in.

4.75 in.

Fig. 18. Size comparison of PalmPilot to Osborne 1.

93 Ibid., 83–84.

94 Moggridge, *Designing Interactions*, 217.

95 Butter and Pogue, *Piloting Palm*, 197.

button size and command placement found ways to minimize the number of stylus taps it would take to proceed from screen to screen.[93]

Palm's first handheld, the Pilot, was launched in February 1996.[94] The device was an instant hit with technology reviewers, who almost unanimously praised the device's speed and ease of use and readily declared religious experiences and feelings of love for the tiny computer. The Pilot sold out faster than Palm could make them, and it won numerous awards. Hawkins's goals had all been met, and each of them had proved to be an important factor in determining the success of the device, demonstrating that he had an innate understanding of the kind of interface experience people desired from PDAs. Palm quickly moved on to a second-generation device, and the renamed PalmPilot would continue the success of the first Pilot. Thousands of developers purchased Palm's software development kit, and a large library of third-party software was quickly made available. Sales remained strong, and by October 1997, one million PalmPilots had been sold in less than eighteen months, making it one of the fastest-selling consumer electronics products up to that time.[95]

Unfortunately, Palm as it was constituted by Hawkins and his team would be short-lived. Problems with the parent company, 3Com, led to the resignation of Hawkins and some of his top executives in 1998. They would go on to form a competing company called Handspring, which became known for its well-designed Treo smartphone line. The two companies would even merge in 2003, but ultimately the types of smartphones and PDAs that Handspring and Palm were creating in the early 2000s suffered with the release of the iPhone in 2007. Multi-touch screens provided an interface experience and level of accessibility that devices based on a stylus and keyboard simply could not match. Nevertheless, the innovations that Palm Computing brought to the field of personal computing have had a lasting impact, and the PalmPilot showed that small form factor personal computing devices were viable if they were well executed.

The Apple iPad—
Touching the Next Era
of Computing

Newsstand

 App Store

 iTunes Store

 Find iPhone

 Game Center

 Settings

 Safari

 Mail

 Music

Since its initial release in 2010, the iPad has become the de facto stand-in for tablet computers. Whether there is something ergonomically pleasing about a device approximately the size of a notepad or a visceral connection to the size of a book or a sheet of paper that reflects centuries of written culture, the tablet has always been something of a sweet spot for interface designers.

However recognizable the iPad is as a tablet device, it is just as notable for its multi-touch screen display. Although the combination of keyboard, mouse, and windows has proved to be a valuable and durable way of interacting with a computer, the idea of just touching a computer and having it do something has always been compelling. As Steve Jobs famously said just before he terminated the Newton project: "God gave us ten styluses. . . . Let's not invent another."[96] In spite of the desire for touchability in computers going as far back as the desire for a tablet, it was not until the release of the iPhone in 2007 that a truly functional touchscreen, with an accompanying operating system, made it into the hands of the majority of computing users (fig. 19). Looking back at the history of these screens and their relationship with the tablet format illustrates why the iPad is such a powerful combination and why it has been labeled the herald for a post-PC era.

96 Walter Isaacson, *Steve Jobs* (New York: Simon & Schuster, 2011), 309.

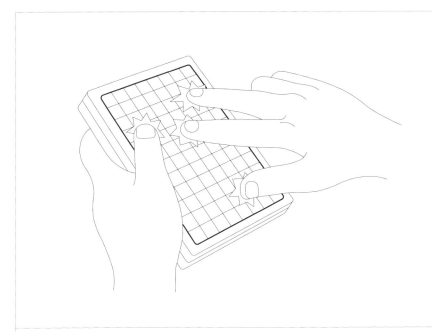

Fig. 19. Diagram showing multi-touch capabilities of Apple's touchscreens.

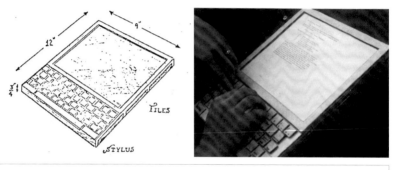

Fig. 20. Alan C. Kay. Drawing and physical mock-up of the DynaBook, 1972. Viewpoints Research Institute.

97   A. Kay and A. Goldberg, "Personal Dynamic Media," *Computer* 10, no. 3 (March 1977): 31–41.

98   Kay himself believes that the iPad does not fully represent the DynaBook, because it lacks the principle of symmetric media. The DynaBook platform was designed to above all promote the creation and sharing of programs and creative works. Kay notes that the iPad is more suited to unidirectional media consumption and that Apple's closed approach to product design is a barrier to truly reaching the potential imagined in the DynaBook. David Greelish, "An Interview with Computing Pioneer Alan Kay," *Time*, April 2, 2013; http://techland.time.com /2013/04/02/an-interview -with-computing-pioneer -alan-kay/.

99   John Sculley, *Odyssey: Pepsi to Apple—A Journey of Adventure, Ideas, and the Future* (New York: Harper & Row, 1987).

One of the earliest tablet-sized computer designs was Alan Kay's DynaBook in 1972 (fig. 20). Kay is responsible for many important inventions in personal computing history, and in fact many of the innovations that came from the Xerox Alto project were developed to support Kay's research into the DynaBook while he was at PARC. Kay devised the DynaBook as part of a project that used the computing practices and needs of children as a foundation for better-informed interface design, and as such the DynaBook was meant to be a device that was accessible to everyone. Along with traditional text editing and data management, the device was a creative medium with which people could not only program, but also create drawings, paintings, animations, and musical compositions. The proposed specifications of the hardware were ambitious for the 1970s, since the design called for an instantaneous response to input, a notebook form factor, a display with a higher resolution than newsprint, and significant storage.[97] Despite the fact that the project never resulted in a salable product, the Dyna-Book predicted many of the features that would make a device like the iPad so successful almost forty years later.[98]

Another iPad-like device that never made it past conceptual design was Apple's Knowledge Navigator, an interactive device that was conceived in 1987 as Apple's vision of the future of personal computing. The Knowledge Navigator project was inspired by ideas from Alan Kay and first described in the book *Odyssey* by John Sculley, then CEO of Apple.[99] In order to demonstrate what the Navigator could do, Sculley commissioned two promotional videos.[100] The Navigator was shaped like a book, which when opened would display a high-resolution touchscreen. The primary way a user interacted with the computer was through conversation with an agent, a dynamic software device with artificial intelligence.[101] Communication with the agent was like talking to a

The Interface Experience—A User's Guide

person, as it could respond to subtle verbal cues and integrate information such as calendar dates, encyclopedia entries, and contacts. The voice-command platforms for iOS and Android—Siri and Google Now—are representative of how agents are being integrated into the experience of interfaces, and the incorporated touch- and voice-controlled agent system of the Knowledge Navigator is slowly becoming part of our computing reality.

Although the DynaBook and Knowledge Navigator were never produced, a number of tablet platforms did precede the iPad. The Linus Write-Top was a tablet-sized PC that used a stylus and had the earliest commercially available handwriting recognition software. Despite being innovative on a number of fronts, the Write-Top was not successful, and only about two thousand units were sold.[102] The first commercially successful tablet was the GRiDPad, released in 1989 by GRiD Systems, the company that had created the first laptop, the GRiD Compass. The GRiDPad, devised by PalmPilot creator Jeff Hawkins, was a well-designed and functional tablet with pen input. However, because of its high price, the device was not widely adopted and was used mostly by large corporations for such purposes as inventory control.[103] AT&T also invested in a short-lived tablet computer called the EO 440 Personal Communicator, which was released in 1992. The EO won awards for its PenPoint software, but it never sold more than ten thousand units and was discontinued in 1994.[104]

The next big increment in tablet-sized computing was the release of Windows XP Tablet PC Edition in 2002, which added pen, handwriting, and speech capabilities to Microsoft's popular XP operating system. Microsoft calls the array of devices designed to work with this operating system Tablet PCs,[105] and they have been developed in a variety of formats. Some open like a laptop; others have more complex mechanisms that allow for the rotation of the screen so that it can be closed over the keyboard for pen input; "slate" versions are closer to the iPad in that they have no keyboard and rely solely on pen input.[106] Tablet PCs have been made by a number of hardware developers, including Acer, Hewlett-Packard, and Compaq, but they have been only moderately successful and do not represent a significant portion of the PC market.

Among the material features of the iPad that have set it apart from the computing devices mentioned so far are the effectiveness and familiarity of the touch experience on the device. As the mouse of the Macintosh and the stylus of the PalmPilot have shown, methods of interacting with a computer that do not involve

100 Apple's Visionary Video: Knowledge Navigator (1987), 2013; http://www.youtube.com/watch?v=m86dJ_15QAQ&feature=youtube_gdata_player.

101 Many interface designers believe agents and responsive artificial intelligence will play an increasingly important role in the way we interact with computers. For more on agents see Brenda Laurel's Computers as Theatre; and Nicholas Negroponte's Being Digital (New York: Knopf, 1995).

102 Steven Stengel, "Linus Write-Top Computer," Obsolete Technology Website, December 10, 2013; http://oldcomputers.net/linus.html.

103 "GRidPad 1910," Computing History; http://www.computinghistory.org.uk/det/6565/gridpad-1910/.

104 Rao, "Early Failures."

105 "Microsoft Tablet PC," Microsoft Developer Network; http://msdn.microsoft.com/en-us/library/ms840465.aspx.

106 "Microsoft Tablet PC," Wikipedia, the Free Encyclopedia, July 22, 2014; http://en.wikipedia.org/w/index.php?title=Microsoft_Tablet_PC&oldid=615448706

107 "HP-150," *Wikipedia, the Free Encyclopedia*, May 21, 2014; http://en.wikipedia.org/w/index.php?title=HP-150&oldid=592406351.

a keyboard have been important in the development of personal computing experiences. Touchscreens have been an oft-debated addition to this array of input alternatives, as some users have bemoaned the width of the finger when compared to the more precise stylus. Nevertheless, such places as the MIT Media Lab experimented with touchscreens in the late 1970s and early 1980s.

In 1983 Hewlett-Packard began selling the first commercial touchscreen personal computer, the HP-150 (fig. 21). The "touching" of the HP-150 was based on infrared sensors that bordered the screen. When you brought your finger close to the screen, the sensors would detect where it was and then estimate what region of the screen you were attempting to touch. The HP-150 did bring Hewlett-Packard a fair bit of success, but the screen was unpredictable and could be used only for simple actions such as selecting large squares. As a result, Hewlett-Packard made the touchscreen an optional add-on in the follow-up HP-150II in 1984 and ceased production of the touch-enabled line of computers soon thereafter.[107]

The product that prepared the way for widespread acceptance of the touchscreen was the iPhone in 2007. What made the iPhone a viable interface was the

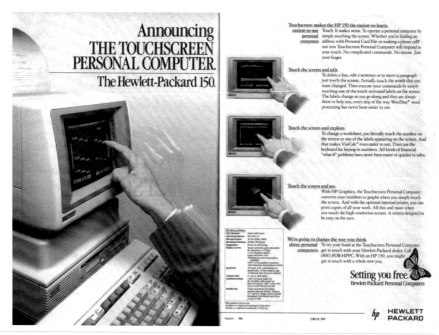

Fig. 21. Hewlett-Packard 150 touchscreen computer advertisement, 1983.

The Interface Experience—A User's Guide

introduction of an accurate multi-touch display and the development of iOS, a mobile operating system that was designed specifically to take advantage of this display. Before the introduction of the iPhone, companies that were manufacturing PDAs and early smartphones, such as Palm, Microsoft, Samsung, Blackberry, and Nokia, continued to use a combination of styluses, buttons, wheels, and keyboards to create a range of interface experiences with varying levels of success. Steve Jobs believed strongly that these various buttons and styluses were inappropriate for the relative scale of the experience of a mobile device. During the unveiling of the iPhone, Jobs said: "Who wants a stylus? . . . We're going to use the best pointing device in the world, we're going to use a pointing device that we're all born with, we're born with ten, we're going to use our fingers."[108]

As with most Apple products, the initial reception of an all-touchscreen device was mixed. Many smartphone keyboard and PDA stylus enthusiasts criticized the lack of a physical keyboard and did not like the fact that, except for power and volume buttons, the iPhone had only one button, the home button. Despite these initial grumblings, the iPhone's integration of the touchscreen and iOS as a coherent and highly functional interface experience radically and rapidly changed the smartphone market. Shortly after the iPhone was released, almost all smartphones adopted the multi-touch screen, and Google's Android was developed as a competing mobile operating system to iOS.

Building on the success of the iPhone and iOS, the development of the iPad (fig. 22) at Apple shifted into high gear over the next few years, although because of the secrecy involved in Apple's product development strategy very few people knew about it. This secrecy is part of Apple's complex culture, and the development, presentation, and initial reception of the iPad tell an interesting story about the role of the corporation in shaping the user's experience and perception of interfaces. Along with his prescience in designing systems that appeal to unfulfilled desires in the computing populace, Steve Jobs was renowned for his often overbearing single-mindedness in developing products. A tablet computer had been percolating at Apple since even before the Knowledge Navigator, and rumors of an iPad-like device being in the works went as far back as 2002.[109] But, as Jobs was wont to do, information about development was kept strictly under wraps because he felt strongly about controlling the perception of a device, particularly its initial release. The creation of this aura of mystique and secrecy heightened excitement for the product's release and generated significant hype even before the product was launched. Apple used this strategy to great effect,

108 Steve Jobs: "Who Wants a Stylus?"—Apple—Steve Jobs at Macworld 2007 in San Francisco, 2010; http://www.youtube.com/watch?v=4YY3MSaUqMg&feature=youtube_gdata_player.

109 Laura June, "The Apple Tablet: A Complete History, Supposedly," Engadget, January 26, 2010; http://www.engadget.com/2010/01/26/the-apple-tablet-a-complete-history-supposedly/.

Fig. 22. Apple. iPad 2, 2011.

110 *Steve Jobs Introduces Original iPad—Apple Special Event (2010)*, 2013; http://www.youtube.com /watch?v=_KN-5zmvjAo.

and the iPad's release is perhaps the best example of how this complex dance of anticipation raises the experience of some interfaces to a different cultural level.

As with many of Apple's product releases, invitations to the event at which the iPad was announced made no specific reference to the device. Nevertheless, the rumor mill had been at work, and people were well aware that the iPad was on its way. The staging and presentation of the events were finely tuned, with Jobs effortlessly presenting not only the products but also the company's justifications for why it believed that its way was the right way to make a product. There was no shortage of hyperbolic mystifying rhetoric. In a typical passage from the presentation, Jobs declared that "using this thing is remarkable, it's so much more intimate than a laptop and it's so much more capable than a smartphone. . . . Watching it is nothing like getting one in your hands, and feeling all of that just right in your hands, right underneath your fingertips."[110]

Jobs was not the only voice deployed in this magical presentation, as Jonathan Ive, Apple's lead designer, almost always made an appearance in promotional videos shown at these events. In the video for the iPad launch he said:

> When something exceeds your ability to understand how it works, it sort of becomes magical, and that's exactly what the iPad is. It's hard to see

how something so thin, so light, could possibly be so capable. . . . The iPad on one hand is clearly way bigger than just a new product, this is a new category, but yet millions and millions of people are going to be instantly familiar with it, they're going to know how to use it. In many ways this defines our vision, our sense of what's next.[111]

111 *iPad Introduction Video (2010)*, 2013; http://www.youtube.com/watch?v=Gho6nCdLpis&feature=youtube_gdata_player.

Ive's voice here is important, because his tone is a reflection of how the company approached the marketing of design after Jobs returned to the company in 1997. The beginning of Ive's influence on the Apple brand can be seen most notably in the Bondi Blue iMac G3 (fig. 23) from 1998.

This radically different-looking computer bucked decades' worth of black, gray, and beige computer cases by utilizing translucent blue plastic instead. From this iconic design, Ive and his team have continually set the standard for personal computing design with the iMac, iPod, iPhone, iPad, and now Apple Watch lines. His presence in the launch event videos is as a sort of guru who embodies and vocalizes a transcendent Apple design ethos, all of which helps to mystify and fetishize these devices more than most other companies do.

Apple sees this kind of product launch as an extension of the user experience. The company believes in controlling the parameters by which people will judge

Fig. 23. Apple. Bondi Blue iMac G3 rear view, 1998.

112 Richard Padilla, "iPad Sales Total 225 Million Units since 2010 as Apple Claims 'Significant Innovation' Coming," *Macrumors*, July 22, 2014; http://www.macrumors.com/2014/07/22/ipad-225-million-sold-significant-innovation/.

113 Steve Lohr, "Is Mr. Gates Pouring Fuel on His Rivals' Fire?," *New York Times*, April 18, 1999; http://www.nytimes.com/1999/04/18/business/economic-view-is-mr-gates-pouring-fuel-on-his-rivals-fire.html.

114 *Steve Jobs and Bill Gates Together in 2007 at D5*, 2012; http://www.youtube.com/watch?v=ZWaX1g_2SSQ&feature=youtube_gdata_player.

115 *Steve Jobs on the Post PC Era*, 2013; http://www.youtube.com/watch?v=YfJ3QxJYsw8&feature=youtube_gdata_player.

their devices. In doing so, Apple hopes to create an aura around them that is both welcoming and awe-inspiring, making the initial use of the interface intimate and personal yet also sensational. As such, the interface experience of Apple computers can be traced back to those initial impressions created through marketing and advertising. The impact of Apple's overall strategy of product development and release has been tremendously effective for the iPad. As of July 2014, 225 million iPads and iPad minis had been sold, making it by far the best-selling tablet platform to date.[112]

Even though many of the technologies that make the iPad an important device are present in the iPhone, the iPad was selected for this project because of its role in what is coming to be called the post-PC era. In personal computing there are two types of products. Generalized devices, like your typical laptop or desktop PC, are platforms for a large number of different computing tasks, from web browsing to video editing to programming. More specialized devices, such as the iPod, iPad, and **Kindle**, come in form factors that are aimed at more specific uses, such as music listening, book reading, and so on. These products are part of the post-PC era, a term coined by MIT computer scientist David Clark,[113] because they are used and approached differently than traditional personal computers.[114]

In an interview in 2010, Steve Jobs made a prediction that reiterated many of the same trends toward mobile, on-your-person devices that Hawkins had foreseen when developing the Zoomer. Jobs likened traditional PCs to trucks and the post-PC devices to cars, and he argued that since America was mostly rural in the early days of the automobile, there were many trucks because vehicles were needed for their functional capabilities in that kind of setting. But as populations grew and people moved into urban settings, cars became more prominent and trucks developed into more utilitarian vehicles owned by fewer people. Jobs believed that the traditional desktop personal computer would not go away completely in this post-PC era, but that fewer people would have a need for them. The majority of computing devices would be the more specialized devices, such as iPhones and iPads, that rely on computing but are not quite as generalized in their capabilities.[115]

The development of the notion of a post-PC era harkens back to something that Donald Norman addressed, the paradox of designing personal computers to do as much as possible. Norman believes that by specializing the design of a device, "it can do its intended job better and more efficiently than powerful, general-purpose machines, at least from the viewpoint of the user. . . . Maybe there is a trade-off here: generality and power versus specialization and ease of use. If so, we ought to examine this carefully. Maybe we need fewer general devices, more specialized ones."[116] The explosion of the many iOS and Android mobile devices and e-readers developed by Amazon, as well as networked information appliances such as the Apple TV, Roku, and Nest thermostat, shows a wide range of devices that seem to fit the post-PC description. The iPad in particular represents the primary transitional object in this shift, as it has convinced people who may have previously been intimidated by their personal computers or were not using their full power to shift to a different kind of interface experience that is more personal, more direct, and easier to use.

That being said, it could also be argued that as the software base of the iPad grows and its functionality expands, it is increasingly more like a PC. This suggests that the distinction between PC and post-PC could ultimately have less to do with whether a device is generalized or specialized and more to do with new material ways of interacting with computers. The term "PC" has come to be historically connected to the windows-and-mouse interface, and the tablet experience differs significantly from that interface. Either way, the discourse surrounding PC versus post-PC is far from resolved, and it will be interesting to see whether the term "post-PC" continues to carry weight within the industry or whether it will even matter anymore that something is or is not a PC. Some have already said that with similar features increasingly spanning a variety of devices, what we are really experiencing is not an era of mobile versus desktop, but rather one of convergence, where many different form factors are being designed to approach a set of common tasks in similar ways.[117] The dance of buzzwords such as "post-PC" and "convergence" are further examples of the high-level rhetorical moves that the various personalities and companies at the center of the computing industry are constantly making. In this way, industry leaders play a never-ending chess match to define and redefine the market in an attempt to convince consumers that they have the best grasp on the future of technology and that they make the devices that most creatively and intimately address the needs of the consuming public.

116 Norman, "Why Interfaces Don't Work," 211.

117 "The Incredibly Short Story of the 'post-PC' Era," *Engadget*; http://www.engadget.com/gallery/the-post-pc-story/.

The Microsoft Kinect— Computing Here, There, Everywhere, but Not There at All

As far back as the era of Bush and Licklider, the concept of the interface has been one that includes the types of input devices that come most naturally to humans: touching, writing, and speaking. The intervening years have seen the introduction and refinement of a number of different physical tools and device-specific operating systems that have tried to make the interface experience more familiar and efficient. Just a few of these various keyboards, mice, styluses, GUIs, and Graffiti-style software have been described in the discussions of the Commodore 64, Macintosh, PalmPilot, and iPad. What most, if not all, of these stages of design represent are accommodations to the inability to create the kind of idealized interface that Bush in particular was hinting at—a system that can intelligently respond to speech cues and simple physical gestures. In no small way, the Kinect (fig. 24) is a first look at how such an interface may change our relationship with computing, and how it would do so by completely removing physical contact with the computer.

118 Alex Pham, "E3: Microsoft Shows Off Gesture Control Technology for Xbox 360," *LA Times Blogs—Technology*, June 1, 2009; http://latimesblogs.latimes.com/technology/2009/06/microsofte3.html.

119 Microsoft announced the successor to its Xbox 360 console, the Xbox One, in 2013. Microsoft introduced the Kinect 2 to work with this new console.

120 Nicole Periroth, "For PrimeSense, Microsoft's Kinect Is Just the Beginning," *Forbes* December 12, 2010; http://www.forbes.com/sites/nicoleperlroth/2010/12/13/for-primesense-microsofts-kinect-is-just-the-beginning/.

Fig. 24. Microsoft. Kinect, first-generation, 2010.

When the Kinect was introduced in 2009, one reporter wrote: "Microsoft kicked off the Electronic Entertainment Expo in Los Angeles this morning by giving the boot to the iconic video game controller."[118] The Kinect was announced as a peripheral to its popular Xbox 360 console that would control the system through voice and gesture. The first iteration of the device[119] was approximately 11 inches long, 3 inches high, and 3 inches deep, and it had to be connected to an Xbox 360, a box the size of an old phonebook, in order to work. The Kinect uses infrared sensors, a color camera, and an array of microphones to allow for motion capture, facial recognition, voice recognition, and video recording and playback. To drive the Kinect, Microsoft licensed chip technology developed by the Israeli company PrimeSense that integrates audio and motion to create 3-D grids that other devices can process.[120] Microsoft then developed a suite of software to integrate PrimeSense's technology with the existing Xbox 360 hardware and software. The announcement of the Kinect was a bold move, particularly coming as it did in the wake of the success of the recently released wireless controllers of the `Nintendo Wii` and Sony's Move system. It represented an important change in the forty years of video game-controller design, a history that has seen numerous generalized and specialty controllers designed to optimize the very physical and real-time experience of interfacing with video games.

The drawing by Damien Lopez in figure 25 shows many different types of video game controllers and illustrates how variable the interface experience has been during the history of home video games. Compared to the relatively small variation in interfaces used in desktop personal computing, where the main differences since the release of the Macintosh have been subtle changes to keyboard and mouse designs, the game controller has seen the coming and going of a plethora of buttons, triggers, dials, sticks, and even gloves. Along with these active interface points, the shape of the body of the controller has changed dramatically. The clunky and often painful rectilinear designs of the `Atari 2600` and `Nintendo Entertainment System (NES)` controllers have given way to more ergonomically designed shapes. The role of the controller's shape and responsiveness is vital to the gaming experience, and to this day gaming platform zealots will argue long into the night about the various merits of the `Sony Playstation's` unique controller body versus the equally distinct curves of Microsoft's design for the Xbox.

The experience of gaming control does not have to take place solely in the hands of the gamer, however, which is what motion-detecting devices like the Kinect are highlighting. Games designed for the Kinect, Wii, and Move are intended to get the gamer up off the couch and make the player space more dynamic. The player space, the physical space in which the player exists, is one of three aspects of experiencing contemporary three-dimensional games. The other two are screen space—the layer occupied by the screen—and 3-D space—the virtual world "behind" the screen created by the graphics of the game. Before motion-detecting controllers were devised, the majority of interaction and motion by the gamer in player space took place within his or her hands and was aimed at providing detailed control of the 3-D space. New devices such as the Kinect and Wii and mimetic controllers for games such as Guitar Hero make much more of the player space active by requiring the use of more or all of the player's body instead of just the hands and eyes. By requiring broader gestures and physical control of the game through arms, shoulders, legs, feet, and even torso and head, these types of games more fully activate the body, and the physical space surrounding the player becomes a greater part of the gaming experience. As such, the interface surface of such games can be an entire room rather than just a controller, and this physical experience means that the sense of play is no longer situated predominantly within the game's digitally rendered 3-D spaces.[121]

Jesper Juul has argued that by more fully activating the player space, detector-based interfaces have increased the potential for game experiences that are more easily accessible. Juul believes that because these gaming experiences are derived from familiar conventions of physical movement that come from outside the video game world, the barrier of entry is lowered and a broader audience will feel more comfortable experimenting with the experience of gaming.[122] The Kinect is aimed at allowing the barrier of entry to be lowered by removing the complexity of modern physical controllers, which is so often an alienating factor in a person's first experience with gaming. The body and voice become the controller, which makes it easier for a complete novice to feel more comfortable stepping into a Kinect gaming experience, despite the lack of any actual physical interaction with the interface.

However, the ease of use of a completely embodied and physical interface such as the Kinect relies heavily on two important factors. First, because there is no object to provide resistance and physical feedback, the device must be very responsive to user movement, so that any lag between user action and system response does not distort the experience of gaming. Second, the design of Kinect-driven games has to negotiate the barrier of actual physical exertion. It takes more energy to play Kinect games (and Wii and Sony Move games), because the gamer is using the whole body, which means more exhaustion and necessarily shorter gaming sessions. Although shorter sessions may encourage more casual gamers to use the system, hard-core gaming communities are less likely to be enthusiastic about changing the long duration and intensely focused nature of their gaming experiences. Concerns about the ability of the Kinect to integrate into established gaming practice have been expressed since its initial launch. Early reviews of the Kinect complained of inaccuracy in the device's controls and bemoaned the lack of tactile feedback and responsiveness that gamers have grown used to with the refined controllers of contemporary

121 Jesper Juul, *A Casual Revolution: Reinventing Video Games and Their Players* (Cambridge, MA: MIT Press, 2010), 16–18.

122 Ibid., 103–19.

Console Standards

 Tandy
1 Stick
1 Button

 Atari 2600
1 Stick
1 Button

Intellivision
1 D-Pad
4 Buttons
1 Number Pad

 ColecoVision
1 Stick
2 Buttons
1 Number Pad

Atari 5200
1 Stick
4 Buttons
3 Options
1 Number Pad

 NES
1 D-Pad
2 Buttons
2 Options

Sega Master System
1 D-Pad
2 Buttons

Genesis
1 D-Pad
3 Buttons
1 Option

TurboGrafx-16
1 D-Pad
2 Buttons
4 Options

SNES
1 D-Pad
4 Buttons
2 Shoulders
2 Options

Sega CD
1 D-Pad
6 Buttons
2 Options

Jaguar
1 D-Pad
3 Buttons
1 Number Pad
2 Options

 3DO
1 D-Pad
3 Buttons
2 Shoulders
2 Options

 Saturn 3D Pad
1 Stick
1 D-Pad
6 Buttons
2 Shoulders
2 Options

 Saturn
1 D-Pad
6 Buttons
2 Shoulders
1 Option

 PS1
1 D-Pad
4 Buttons
4 Shoulders
2 Options

 N64
1 D-Pad
1 Stick
6 Buttons
3 Shoulders
1 Option

 PS1 Dual Shock
1 D-Pad
2 Click Sticks
4 Buttons
4 Shoulders
3 Options

 Dreamcast
1 D-Pad
1 Stick
4 Buttons
2 Shoulders
1 Option

 Playstation 2
1 D-Pad
2 Click Sticks
4 Buttons
4 Shoulders
3 Options

X-Box Old
1 D-Pad
2 Click Sticks
6 Buttons
4 Shoulders
2 Options

Gamecube
1 D-Pad
2 Sticks
4 Buttons
3 Shoulders
1 Option

X-Box New
1 D-Pad
2 Click Sticks
6 Buttons
2 Shoulders
2 Options

X-Box 360
1 D-Pad
2 Click Sticks
4 Buttons
4 Shoulders
3 Options

 PS3
1 D-Pad
2 Click Sticks
4 Buttons
4 Shoulders
2 Sticks
3 Options
Motion Sensitive

 Wii Mote
1 Stick
2 Shoulders
Motion Sensitive
Aimed

1 D-Pad
3 Buttons
1 Shoulder
4 Options
Motion Sensitive
Aimed

Wii Arcade
1 D-Pad
2 Sticks
4 Buttons
4 Shoulders
3 Options

 WiiU
1 D-Pad
2 Click Sticks
4 Buttons
4 Shoulders
5 Options
1 Touch Screen
1 Stylus
1 Camera
1 Microphone
Motions Sensitive
Aimed
Near Field Communication

 PS4
1 D-Pad
2 Click Sticks
4 Buttons
4 Shoulders
1 Touchpad
3 Options
Motion Sensitive

 X-Box One
1 D-Pad
2 Click Sticks
4 Buttons
2 Shoulders
3 Options

Specialty Controllers

Atari Tennis
1 Knob
1 Button

 ColecoVision
1 Stick
4 Buttons
1 Number Pad
1 Scroll Wheel

Atari Kid's Controller
1 Number Pad

 Atari Video Touch Pad
1 Number Pad

 PS3 Motion
4 Buttons
1 Trigger
4 Options
Motion Sensitive

NES Power Glove
1 D-Pad
2 Buttons
15 Options
Motion Sensitive
Aimed

NES U Force
Motion Sensitive
8 Options

Dreamcast Fission
1 Stick
4 Buttons
1 Reel
1 Option
Motion Sensitive

 R.O.B.
2 Hands
2 Disks
2 Levers
Aimed

SNES Super Scope
1 Button
2 Options
Aimed

 PS2 Guitar
5 Buttons
2 Options
1 Strum
1 Wammy
Motion Sensitive

 360 DJ Hero
1 D-Pad
8 Buttons
2 Options
1 Turntable
1 Dial
1 Crossfader

NES Light Gun
1 Button
Aimed

Master System Light Phaser
1 Button
Aimed

Saturn Virtua Gun
2 Buttons
Aimed

Playstation GunCon
3 Buttons
Aimed

Keyboard and Mouse
110 Keys
2 Number Pads

2 Buttons
1 Scroll Wheel
Motion Sensitive

N64 Mic.
1 Microphone

Game Cube Mic.
1 Button
1 Microphone

Game Cube Keyboard
81 Keys
1 D-Pad
2 Sticks
4 Buttons
3 Shoulders
1 Option

Rock Band (360)

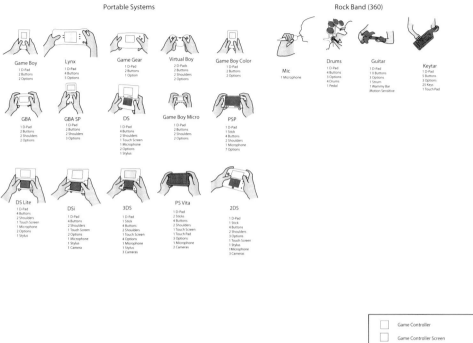

Portable Systems

Game Boy
1 D-Pad
2 Buttons
2 Options

Lynx
1 D-Pad
4 Buttons
5 Options

Game Gear
1 D-Pad
2 Buttons
1 Option

Virtual Boy
2 D-Pads
2 Buttons
2 Shoulders
2 Options

Game Boy Color
1 D-Pad
2 Buttons
2 Options

GBA
1 D-Pad
2 Buttons
2 Shoulders
2 Options

GBA SP
1 D-Pad
2 Buttons
2 Shoulders
3 Options

DS
1 D-Pad
4 Buttons
2 Shoulders
1 Touch Screen
1 Microphone
2 Options
1 Stylus

Game Boy Micro
1 D-Pad
2 Buttons
2 Shoulders
2 Options

PSP
1 D-Pad
1 Stick
4 Buttons
2 Shoulders
2 Microphone
7 Options

DS Lite
1 D-Pad
4 Buttons
2 Shoulders
1 Touch Screen
1 Microphone
2 Options
1 Stylus

DSi
1 D-Pad
4 Buttons
2 Shoulders
1 Touch Screen
2 Options
1 Microphone
1 Stylus
1 Camera

3DS
1 D-Pad
1 Stick
4 Buttons
2 Shoulders
1 Touch Screen
4 Options
1 Microphone
1 Stylus
3 Cameras

PS Vita
1 D-Pad
2 Sticks
4 Buttons
2 Shoulders
1 Touch Screen
1 Touch Pad
3 Options
1 Microphone
2 Cameras

2DS
1 D-Pad
1 Stick
4 Buttons
2 Shoulders
2 Options
1 Touch Screen
1 Stylus
1 Microphone
3 Cameras

Rock Band (360)

Mic
1 Microphone

Drums
1 D-Pad
4 Buttons
3 Options
4 Drums
1 Pedal

Guitar
1 D-Pad
1 0 Buttons
3 Options
1 Strum
1 Wammy Bar
Motion Sensitive

Keytar
1 D-Pad
5 Buttons
3 Options
25 Keys
1 Touch Pad

Game Controller

Game Controller Screen

Hand

Input Device of Controller

D-Pad -	Up, Down, Left, Right
Stick -	360° Control
Button -	A, B, C, X, Y, Z
Option -	Start, Select, Mode, Pause
Shoulder -	L, R, Z
Number Pad -	1-9, #, *
Motion Sensitive	
Aimed	
Touch Screen	
Microphone	
Camera	

Fig. 25. Damien Lopez. *A History of Game Controllers*, 2015. Courtesy of the artist.

123 Ben Kuchera, "Buy a House, Clean Your Floor, Move Your Butt: Ars Reviews Kinect," *Ars Technica*, November 4, 2010; http://arstechnica.com /gaming/reviews/2010/11 /buy-a-house-clean-your-floor -move-your-butt-ars-reviews -kinect.ars.

gaming systems.[123] As a result, the ultimate fate of the device as a driving force for sales of the Xbox console remains somewhat in doubt.

Although the Kinect is a significant part of the evolution of the video game controller, it is also part of another trend in personal computing, which involves moving the user's interaction with the Internet and cloud-based services into the living room and onto television screens. The battle for the living room is one that many companies, including Apple, Microsoft, Sony, and Google, have entered. Recognizing that personal computing devices have increasingly become conduits for media experiences that were once the purview of more specialized technologies, such as cable boxes, VCRs, and DVD players, these companies are looking for a way to bring the living room experience of television, movies, and music into their ecosystems. It is in this context that voice control, one of the simpler features of the Kinect, is also one of its most useful.

The Kinect predominantly enhances games through motion-gesture control, but its voice controls can be used to navigate through the Xbox's dashboard and to control a variety of streaming services that come through the device. Being able to say verbal commands such as "Play," "Stop," or "Netflix" enables a user to control the Xbox without the need to fumble for a misplaced remote. This is one of the Kinect's most intuitive features. I noticed this in my own personal life soon after our son was born. I was able to hold him in my arms and give him a bottle while being able to control Netflix content with my voice. After enough use, I soon started to notice the lack of voice control in other devices, and I realized how easy the Kinect made it to navigate menus and call up commands. Now that my son is interested in watching *Sesame Street*, he too has quickly noticed the ease with which the Kinect can control the Xbox, as he tries in vain to get the device to respond to him by shouting commands at it.

Making the media viewing experience more accessible and unique is important for Microsoft. The company is relying on the Xbox family of consoles to be the central platform for providing access to services such as Netflix, Amazon Prime, HBO Go, and perhaps someday soon cable subscriptions. The recently released successor to the Xbox 360, the Xbox One in particular was designed to encompass more fully a media delivery strategy that Microsoft had incrementally been implementing with 360 and across its other platforms. The unifying aesthetic of this cross-device strategy can be seen in the Metro design schema, which originally debuted with Windows 8 but now determines the look of all its platforms, including its smartphones and the Xbox operating systems. A similar design strategy can be seen in Apple's increased unification of iOS, the Macintosh operating system, and the Apple TV. Within this evolving competition for control of the living room experience, the Kinect was meant to be the peripheral that distinguished Microsoft's product from other gaming platforms such as Sony's (the PS4) and Nintendo's (the Wii) that were adding similar functionality. It was also meant to get Microsoft out ahead of non-gaming competitors, such as Apple, which is rumored to be integrating iPhone-like Siri voice control into its Apple TV, and Google, which is integrating Google Now voice control into its Chromecast media device. The success or failure of this new type of interface in the very personal computing space of the living room is, therefore, very important to Microsoft, and the firm's ability to transition users successfully to an Xbox-centered and possibly Kinect-controlled interface experience will greatly impact the success of its living room strategy.

Of the five objects discussed, the long-term impact of the Kinect is by far the most uncertain. This motion- and voice-sensing technology, designed as a peripheral to Microsoft's popular Xbox 360 console, has been available to consumers only since November 2010, and it has in the ensuing four years suffered ebbs and flows in its popularity. The original Kinect sold more than 8 million units in the first sixty days after its launch, breaking the records set by the iPhone and iPad for fastest-selling consumer electronics device.[124] By early 2013, the first Kinect had sold over 24 million units,[125] and Xbox One purchases with the bundled Kinect 2 sold more than 5 million units in their first year of availability.[126] Nevertheless, it is unclear how many of those purchases are in regular use, and there is a great deal of skepticism in gaming communities as to the ultimate utility of the Kinect devices. In addition, the development of Kinect-specific games has waned after an initial spike. It remains to be seen whether the new Kinect on the Xbox One will be a differentiator in the living room, or a complex oddity that in the end proves to be more of an obstacle for Microsoft to negotiate in its product strategy. The investment in the technology is there, however, and companies believe that they can leverage gestural technology in future devices. After licensing the 3-D chip from PrimeSense for the first Kinect, Microsoft saw enough potential in 3-D gesture control to move all development in-house for the Xbox One's improved Kinect. PrimeSense was subsequently acquired by Apple in 2013, signaling that there may be Kinect-like applications built into devices such as Macs, iPhones, iPads, and most notably, the Apple TV.[127]

124 Nick Bilton, "Microsoft Sells 10 Million Kinects, Breaking Record," *Bits Blog*, March 9, 2011; http://bits.blogs. nytimes.com/2011/03/09 /microsoft-sells-10-million -kinects-breaking-record/.

125 Zach Epstein, "Microsoft Says Xbox 360 Sales Have Surpassed 76 Million Units, Kinect Sales Top 24 Million," *BGR*, February 12, 2013; http://bgr .com/2013/02/12/microsoft -xbox-360-sales-2013–325481/.

126 Kyle Orland, "Microsoft: Xbox One Sales Double in US Following Kinect Unbundling," *Ars Technica*, July 17, 2014; http://arstechnica.com /gaming/2014/07/microsoft -xbox-one-sales-double-in-us -following-kinect-unbundling/.

127 Charles Arthur, "Why Did Apple Buy PrimeSense? For a Key Technology It'll Deploy within a Year," *The Guardian*, November 25, 2013, sec. Technology; http://www. theguardian.com /technology/2013/nov /25/why-did-apple -buy-primesense-for-a-key -technology-itll-deploy -within-a-year.

The physical decoupling of the human from the machine represents a significant shift. It remains to be seen if the Kinect will be as successful in ushering in a new experience as the PalmPilot was, or whether the Kinect will ultimately turn out to be an unfulfilled precursor to a more refined device to come, like the Newton. Either way, the development of the Kinect represents a major expansion in the sensory and spatial possibilities of the experience of personal computing.

Bibliography

1984 Apple's Macintosh Commercial (HD), 2012. http://www.youtube.com/watch?v=Vtvjbmo
    Dx-I&feature=youtube_gdata_player.

Alan Kay: Doing with Images Makes Symbols Pt 1. University Video Communications, 1987.
    http://archive.org/details/AlanKeyD1987.

Andre, Bartley K., Daniel J. Coster, Daniele De Iuliis, Richard P. Howarth, Jonathan P. Ive, Steve Jobs,
    Shin Nishibori, et al. "United States Patent: D504889—Electronic Device," May 10, 2005.
    http://patft.uspto.gov/netacgi/nph-Parser?Sect1=PTO1&Sect2=HITOFF&d=PALL&p=1&u
    =%2Fnetahtml%2FPTO%2Fsrchnum.htm&r=1&f=G&l=50&s1=D504,889.PN.&OS=PN
    /D504,889&RS=PN/D504,889.

"Apple Computer, Inc. v. Microsoft Corp." *Wikipedia, the Free Encyclopedia*, August 13, 2014.
    http://en.wikipedia.org/w/index.php?title=Apple_Computer,_Inc._v._Microsoft
    _Corp.&oldid=613954034.

AppleInsider Staff. "Steve Jobs Squashes Rumors of Smaller, 7-Inch iPad from Apple." *AppleInsider*,
    October 18, 2010. http://appleinsider.com/articles/10/10/18/steve_jobs_squashes_rumors
    _of_smaller_7_inch_ipad.

Apple's Visionary Video: Knowledge Navigator (1987), 2013. http://www.youtube.com/watch?v
    =m86dJ_15QAQ&feature=youtube_gdata_player.

Arrington, Michael. "The Unauthorized TechCrunch iPad Review." *TechCrunch*, April 2, 2010.
    http://techcrunch.com/2010/04/02/the-unauthorized-techcrunch-ipad-review/.

Arthur, Charles. "Why Did Apple Buy PrimeSense? For a Key Technology It'll Deploy within a Year."
    The Guardian, November 25, 2013, sec. Technology. http://www.theguardian.com
    /technology/2013/nov/25/why-did-apple-buy-primesense-for-a-key-technology-itll-deploy
    -within-a-year.

Asavin, Wattanajantra. "Steve Jobs Thinks Your Fingers Are Too Fat for 7-Inch Tablets." *CNET*,
    October 19, 2010. http://www.cnet.com/news/steve-jobs-thinks-your-fingers-are-too-fat-for
    -7-inch-tablets/.

Bagnall, Brian. *Commodore: A Company on the Edge.* Winnipeg, MB: Variant Press, 2010.

Bardini, Thierry. *Bootstrapping: Douglas Engelbart, Coevolution, and the Origins of Personal
    Computing.* Writing Science. Stanford, CA: Stanford University Press, 2000.

Baudrillard, Jean. "Xerox and Infinity." In *The Transparency of Evil: Essays on Extreme Phenomena*,
    translated by James Benedict, 51–60. London and New York: Verso, 1993.

"BBC News—Ex-Apple Boss Sculley Sets Record Straight on Jobs." http://www.bbc.com/news
    /technology-16538745.

Berkes, Otto. "iPad." *Otto Berkes' Weblog*, January 27, 2010. http://ottoberkes.wordpress.com/2010
    /01/27/ipad/.

Berry, David M. *Critical Theory and the Digital.* New York: Bloomsbury, 2014.

Beyer, Christian. "Edmund Husserl." In *The Stanford Encyclopedia of Philosophy*, edited by Edward N. Zalta. Stanford, CA: Stanford University Press, 2013. http://plato.stanford.edu /archives/win2013/entries/husserl/.

Bharucha, Rehan. "Working of Microsoft's PrimeSense Technology Based Kinect—An Elaboration— TechNet Articles—United States (English)—TechNet Wiki." *Microsoft TechNet*, December 27, 2011. http://social.technet.microsoft.com/wiki/contents/articles/6370.working-of-microsoft -s-primesense-technology-based-kinect-an-elaboration.aspx.

Bilton, Nick. "Microsoft Sells 10 Million Kinects, Breaking Record." *Bits Blog*, March 9, 2011. http:// bits.blogs.nytimes.com/2011/03/09/microsoft-sells-10-million-kinects-breaking-record/.

Bosker, Bianca. "Apple's 'iPad 2' Won't Be a Smaller, 7-Inch Version, Steve Jobs Suggests." *Huffington Post*, October 19, 2010. http://www.huffingtonpost.com/2010/10/19/apples-ipad -2-wont-be-a-s_n_767882.html.

Brecht, Bertolt. "The Modern Theatre Is the Epic Theatre." In *Brecht on Theatre: The Development of an Aesthetic*, 33–42. London: Methuen, 1964.

Bricklin, Dan. "About Tablet Computing Old and New." *Dan Bricklin's Web Site*, November 22, 2002. http://www.bricklin.com/tabletcomputing.htm.

Bulik, Beth Snyder. "Marketer of the Decade: Apple." *Advertising Age*, October 18, 2010. http://adage.com/article/special-report-marketer-of-the-year-2010/marketer-decade -apple/146492/.

Burrows, Peter. "Apple Shifts TV Ads In-House as Chiat/Day Rift Widens." *Bloomberg*, June 4, 2014. http://www.bloomberg.com/news/2014-06-04/apple-shifts-tv-ads-in-house-as-chiat-day -rift-widens.html.

Bush, Vannevar. "As We May Think." *Atlantic Monthly*, July 1945.

———. "As We May Think." *Life*, September 1945.

Butter, Andrea, and David Pogue. *Piloting Palm: The Inside Story of Palm, Handspring, and the Birth of the Billion-Dollar Handheld Industry*. Hoboken, NJ: Wiley, 2002.

Campbell-Kelly, Martin, William Aspray, Nathan Ensmenger, and Jeffrey R. Yost. *Computer: A History of the Information Machine*. New York: Westview Press, 2013.

Cantsin, Monty. "Against the Frictionless Interface! An Interview with Lori Emerson." *Furtherfield*, July 23, 2014. http://furtherfield.org/features/interviews/against-frictionless-interface -interview-lori-emerson.

Ceruzzi, Paul E. *A History of Modern Computing*. Cambridge, MA: MIT Press, 2003.

ComputerHistory. *Commodore 64—25th Anniversary Celebration*, 2007. http://www.youtube.com /watch?v=NBvbsPNBIyk&feature=youtube_gdata_player.

"Computing History Timeline." *Computing History*. http://www.computinghistory.org.uk/cgi /computing-timeline.pl.

Dougherty, Philip H. "Advertising; Apple and Newsweek Special." *New York Times*, November 7, 1984, sec. Business. http://www.nytimes.com/1984/11/07/business/advertising-apple-and -newsweek-special.html.

Dourish, Paul. *Where the Action Is: The Foundations of Embodied Interaction*. Cambridge, MA: MIT Press, 2001.

Drucker, Johanna. *Graphesis: Visual Forms of Knowledge Production*. MetaLABprojects. Cambridge, MA: Harvard University Press, 2014.

———. "Humanities Approaches to Interface Theory." *Culture Machine* 12, February 18, 2011. http://www.culturemachine.net/index.php/cm/article/view/434.

———. "Performative Materiality and Theoretical Approaches to Interface." *Digital Humanities Quarterly* 7, no. 1 (2013). http://www.digitalhumanities.org/dhq/vol/7/1/000143 /000143.html.

Edwards, Benj. "Inside the Commodore 64." *PCWorld*, November 4, 2008. http://www.pcworld .com/article/152528/comm64.html.

———. "[Retro Scan of the Week] The HP-150 Touchscreen Computer." *Vintage Computing and Gaming: Adventures in Classic Technology*, August 20, 2007. http://www .vintagecomputing.com/index.php/archives/356/retro-scan-of-the-week-the-hp-150 -touchscreen-computer.

———. "The 10 Worst PC Keyboards of All Time." *PCWorld*, November 1, 2007. http://www.pcworld.com/article/139100/the_10_worst_pc_keyboards_of_all _time.html.

Emerson, Lori. *Reading Writing Interfaces: From the Digital to the Bookbound*. Electronic Mediations 44. Minneapolis: University of Minnesota Press, 2014.

"Emulator." *Wikipedia, the Free Encyclopedia*, July 28, 2014. http://en.wikipedia.org/w/index.php ?title=Emulator&oldid=618746836.

Engelbart, Douglas C. "Augmenting Human Intellect: A Conceptual Framework." *Doug Engelbart Institute*, October 1962. http://www.dougengelbart.org/pubs/augment-3906.html.

Engelbart, Douglas C., et al. *Advanced Intellect-Augmentation Techniques*. Menlo Park, CA: Stanford Research Institute, 1970. http://archive.org/details/bitsavers_sriarcAdvatation TechniquesJul70_10025402.

Epstein, Zach. "Microsoft Says Xbox 360 Sales Have Surpassed 76 Million Units, Kinect Sales Top 24 Million." *BGR*, February 12, 2013. http://bgr.com/2013/02/12/microsoft-xbox-360 -sales-2013-325481/.

"Erik S. Klein's Vintage Computer Collection—Home of Historical Computers Such as Mark-8, Altair, Kenbak, Apple, Commodore and IBM as Well as the VC Forum, VCGM (Marketplace) and the VC Wiki." http://www.vintage-computer.com/index.shtml.

Esslinger, Hartmut, and Florian Hufnagl. *Keep It Simple: The Early Design Years of Apple*. Stuttgart: Arnoldsche Art Publishers, 2013.

"The First Thirty Years." *TBWA CHIAT DAY NY*. http://tbwachiatdayny.com/.

Fried, Ina. "Steve Jobs at D8: Post-PC Era Is Nigh." *CNET*, June 1, 2010. http://www.cnet.com /news/steve-jobs-at-d8-post-pc-era-is-nigh/.

Galloway, Alexander R. *The Interface Effect*. Cambridge and Boston: Polity, 2012.

Gideon, Tim. "Apple iPad Review." *PCMAG*, March 31, 2010. http://www.pcmag.com /article2/0,2817,2362040,00.asp.

Golson, Jordan. "Steve Jobs' First Public Demonstration of the Macintosh, Hidden since 1984." http:// www.macrumors.com/2014/01/26/macintosh-introduction-boston-computer-society/.

Grätz, Ina. *Apple Design*. Ostfildern and Berlin: Hatje Cantz, 2011.

Greelish, David. "An Interview with Computing Pioneer Alan Kay." *Time*, April 2, 2013. http://techland. time.com/2013/04/02/an-interview-with-computing-pioneer-alan-kay/.

"GRidPad 1910." *Computing History*. http://www.computinghistory.org.uk/det/6565/gridpad-1910/.

Hachman, Mark. "A History of Windows Tablets." *PCMAG*, October 17, 2012. http://www.pcmag .com/slideshow/story/304004/a-history-of-windows-tablets.

Hahn, Brian K. "The Tandy ZOOMER, ZPDA." *8bit Micro.com*, 2005. http://www.8bit-micro.com /tandy-zoomer-z-pda.htm.

Halimi, Natalie. "A Lesson in Entrepreneurship from MIT's Nicholas Negroponte." *Similar Web Blog*, December 24, 2013. http://blog.similarweb.com/a-lesson-in-entrepreneurship-from-mits -nicholas-negroponte/.

Harwood, John. *The Interface: IBM and the Transformation of Corporate Design, 1945/1976*. A Quadrant Book. Minneapolis: University of Minnesota Press, 2011.

Hertzfeld, Andy. *Revolution in the Valley: The Insanely Great Story of How the Mac Was Made*. Beijing and Sebastopol, CA: O'Reilly Media, 2004.

"Hewlett-Packard-150 Touchscreen Personal Computer with Hewlett-Packard 9121 Dual Drives, 1983." *HP Virtual Museum*. http://www.hp.com/hpinfo/abouthp/histnfacts/museum/personalsystems/0031/.

Hiltzik, Michael A. *Dealers of Lightning: Xerox PARC and the Dawn of the Computer Age*. New York: HarperBusiness, 1999.

Hookway, Branden. *Interface*. Cambridge, MA: MIT Press, 2014.

Hormby, Tim. "The Story behind Apple's Newton." *Low End Mac*, August 6, 2013. http://lowendmac .com/2013/the-story-behind-apples-newton/.

"HP-150." *Wikipedia, the Free Encyclopedia*, May 21, 2014. http://en.wikipedia.org/w/index. php?title=HP-150&oldid=592406351.

"HP Computer Museum." http://www.hpmuseum.net/display_item.php?hw=43.

Huhtamo, Erkki. "From Cybernation to Interaction: A Contribution to an Archaeology of Interactivity." In *The Digital Dialectic: New Essays on New Media*, edited by Peter Lunenfeld, 96–110. Leonardo Series. Cambridge, MA: MIT Press, 1999.

Husserl, Edmund. *Experience and Judgment*. Evanston, IL: Northwestern University Press, 1973.

Hutchins, Edwin L., James D. Hollan, and Donald A. Norman. "Direct Manipulation Interfaces." *Hum.-Comput. Interact.* 1, no. 4 (December 1985): 311–38. doi:10.1207/s15327051hci0104_2.

"iMac Intel 27" EMC 2639 Teardown." *iFixit*. https://www.ifixit.com/Teardown/iMac+Intel+27 -Inch+EMC+2639+Teardown/17828.

"The Incredibly Short Story of the 'Post-PC' Era." *Engadget*. http://www.engadget.com/gallery /the-post-pc-story/.

"Interface." *Oxford Dictionaries*. Oxford: Oxford University Press. http://www.oxforddictionaries .com/us/definition/american_english/interface.

"Interfacing." *Wikipedia, the Free Encyclopedia*, July 5, 2014. http://en.wikipedia.org/w/index.php ?title=Interfacing&oldid=541144576.

iPad Introduction Video (2010), 2013. http://www.youtube.com/watch?v=Gho6nCdLpis&feature =youtube_gdata_player.

Isaacson, Walter. *Steve Jobs*. New York: Simon & Schuster, 2011.

Jack Tramiel "Computers for the Masses Not the Classes" (Δεκέμβριος, 1995), 2012. https://www .youtube.com/watch?v=G7rUWVfS01M&feature=youtube_gdata_player.

Jardin, Xeni. "Review: Apple's iPad Is a Touch of Genius." *Boing Boing*, March 31, 2010. http:// boingboing.net/2010/03/31/a-first-look-at-ipad.html.

Johnson, Steven. "Marrying Tech and Art." *Wall Street Journal*, August 27, 2011, sec. Life and Style. http://online.wsj.com/news/articles/SB10001424053111904875404576532342684923826 ?mg=reno64-wsj.

June, Laura. "The Apple Tablet: A Complete History, Supposedly." *Engadget*, January 26, 2010. http://www.engadget.com/2010/01/26/the-apple-tablet-a-complete-history-supposedly/.

jupiter2. "Apple Advertising and Brochure Gallery 3." *The Mothership*, 1984. http://www .macmothership.com/gallery/gallery3.html.

Juul, Jesper. *A Casual Revolution: Reinventing Video Games and Their Players*. Cambridge, MA: MIT Press, 2010.

Kahney, Leander. *The Cult of Mac*. San Francisco: No Starch Press, 2004.

———. "John Sculley on Steve Jobs, the Full Interview Transcript." *Cult of Mac*, October 14, 2010. http://www.cultofmac.com/63295/john-sculley-on-steve-jobs-the-full-interview-transcript/.

Kay, Alan. "A Personal Computer for Children of All Ages." In *Proceedings of the ACM Annual Conference—Volume 1*. ACM '72. New York: ACM, 1972. doi:10.1145/800193.1971922.

———. "User Interface: A Personal View." In *The Art of Human-Computer Interface Design*, edited by Brenda Laurel and S. Joy Mountford, 191–207. Reading, MA: Addison-Wesley, 1990.

Kay, Alan, and Adele Goldberg. "Personal Dynamic Media." *Computer* 10, no. 3 (March 1977): 31–41. doi:10.1109/C-M.1977.217672.

"Kinect for Xbox 360 Hits Million Mark in Just 10 Days." *Microsoft News Center*, November 15, 2010. https://www.microsoft.com/en-us/news/press/2010/nov10/11-15ninemillionpr.aspx.

Kingery, W. D. "Technological Systems and Some Implications with Regard to Continuity and Change." In *History from Things: Essays on Material Culture*, edited by Steven D. Lubar and W. D. Kingery, 215–30. Washington, DC: Smithsonian Institution Press, 1993.

Kittler, Friedrich A. "There Is No Software." *Ctheory.net*, October 18, 1995, a032.

Kittler, Friedrich A., and Sara Ogger. "Computer Graphics: A Semi-Technical Introduction." *Grey Room*, no. 2 (January 1, 2001): 31–45.

Kuchera, Ben. "Buy a House, Clean Your Floor, Move Your Butt: Ars Reviews Kinect." *Ars Technica*, November 4, 2010. http://arstechnica.com/gaming/reviews/2010/11/buy-a-house-clean-your-floor-move-your-butt-ars-reviews-kinect.ars.

Kuehl, Julie, and John Martellaro. "John Sculley: The Truth about Me, Apple, and Steve Jobs, Part 1." *Mac Observer*, January 13, 2012. http://www.macobserver.com/tmo/article/john_sculley_the_full_transcript_part1.

———. "John Sculley: The Truth about Me, Apple, and Steve Jobs, Part 2." *Mac Observer*, January 13, 2012. http://www.macobserver.com/tmo/article/john_sculley_the_full_transcript_part2/.

Laurel, Brenda. *Computers as Theatre*. Reading, MA: Addison-Wesley, 1993.

Laurel, Brenda, and S. Joy Mountford, eds. *The Art of Human-Computer Interface Design*. Reading, MA: Addison-Wesley, 1990.

Lee, Nicole. "Life after Kinect: PrimeSense's Plans for a Post-Microsoft Future." *Engadget*, June 21, 2013. http://www.engadget.com/2013/06/21/life-after-kinect-primesense-post-microsoft/.

LEM Staff. "Mac Plus." *Low End Mac*. http://lowendmac.com/1986/mac-plus/.

Leonardi, Paul M. "Digital Materiality? How Artifacts without Matter, Matter." *First Monday* 15, no. 6 (2010). http://firstmonday.org/ojs/index.php/fm/article/view/3036.

Levy, Steven. *Insanely Great: The Life and Times of Macintosh, the Computer That Changed Everything*. New York: Penguin Books, 2000.

Licklider, J. C. R. "Man-Computer Symbiosis." In *The NewMediaReader*, edited by Noah Wardrip-Fruin and Nick Montfort, 74–82. Cambridge, MA: MIT Press, 2003.

Lohr, Steve. "Is Mr. Gates Pouring Fuel on His Rivals' Fire?" *New York Times*, April 18, 1999. http://www.nytimes.com/1999/04/18/business/economic-view-is-mr-gates-pouring-fuel-on-his-rivals-fire.html.

MacIntosh Manuals, 2012. http://www.youtube.com/watch?v=AAK3hPOLBAY&feature=youtube_gdata_player.

Manovich, Lev. *The Language of New Media*. Cambridge, MA: MIT Press, 2002. http://www.manovich.net/LNM/Manovich.pdf.

Markhoff, John, and Ezra Shapiro. "Macintosh's Other Designers." *BYTE*, August 1984.

Mattern, Shannon. "Interface Critique." *Words in Space*. http://www.wordsinspace.net/wordpress/2014/01/10/interface-critique/.

Matthews, Ian. "Commodore 64—The Best Selling Computer in History." *Commodore Computers: VIC20 C64 PET C128 Plus4—All 8 Bit Machines*. http://www.commodore.ca/commodore-products/commodore-64-the-best-selling-computer-in-history/.

McKenzie, Jon. *Perform or Else: From Discipline to Performance*. London and New York: Routledge, 2001.

McWilliams, Chandler B. "The Other Software." *Digital Arts and Culture* 2009 (conference), December 12, 2009. http://escholarship.org/uc/item/3vg159kn.

Mesa, Andy. "Apple IIe." *The Apple Museum*. http://applemuseum.bott.org/sections/computers/IIe.html.

"Microsoft Tablet PC." *Microsoft Developer Network*. http://msdn.microsoft.com/en-us/library
/ms840465.aspx.

"Microsoft Tablet PC." *Wikipedia, the Free Encyclopedia*, July 22, 2014. http://en.wikipedia.org/w
/index.php?title=Microsoft_Tablet_PC&oldid=615448706.

Moggridge, Bill. *Designing Interactions*. Cambridge, MA: MIT Press, 2007.

Mossberg, Walt. "Apple iPad Review: Laptop Killer? Pretty Close." *AllThingsD*, March 31, 2010.
http://allthingsd.com/20100331/apple-ipad-review/.

"Most Important Companies," *Byte*, September 1995.

Mui, Chunka. "How Apple Invented the Future (and the iPad) in 1986." *Forbes*, October 24, 2011.
http://www.forbes.com/sites/chunkamui/2011/10/24/for-a-preview-of-the-ipad3-watch-this
-23-year-old-apple-video/2/.

Murray, Janet H. *Inventing the Medium: Principles of Interaction Design as a Cultural Practice*.
Cambridge, MA: MIT Press, 2012.

Negroponte, Nicholas. *Being Digital*. New York: Alfred A. Knopf, 1995.

Norman, Donald A. "Affordances and Design." *Jnd.org*. http://www.jnd.org/dn.mss/affordances
_and.html.

———. "Cognitive Artifacts." In *Designing Interaction: Psychology at the Human-Computer
Interface*, edited by John Millar Carroll, 4:17–38. Cambridge Series on Human-Computer
Interaction. Cambridge: Cambridge University Press, 1991.

———. *The Design of Everyday Things*. New York: Doubleday, 1990.

———. *The Invisible Computer: Why Good Products Can Fail, the Personal Computer Is So
Complex, and Information Appliances Are the Solution*. Cambridge, MA: MIT Press, 1998.

———. "Why Interfaces Don't Work." In *The Art of Human-Computer Interface Design*, edited by
Brenda Laurel and S. Joy Mountford, 209–19. Reading, MA: Addison-Wesley, 1990.

Orland, Kyle. "Microsoft: Xbox One Sales Double in US Following Kinect Unbundling." *Ars Technica*,
July 17, 2014. http://arstechnica.com/gaming/2014/07/microsoft-xbox-one-sales-double-in
-us-following-kinect-unbundling/.

Paczkowski, John. "iPad Death Watch." *AAPL Investors.net*, January 27, 2014. http://aaplinvestors
.net/stats/ipad/ipaddeathwatch/.

Padilla, Richard. "iPad Sales Total 225 Million Units since 2010 as Apple Claims 'Significant
Innovation' Coming." *Macrumors*, July 22, 2014. http://www.macrumors.com/2014/07/22
/ipad-225-million-sold-significant-innovation/.

Pang, Alex Soojung-Kim. "The Xerox PARC Visit." *Making the Macintosh: Technology and Culture in
Silicon Valley*. http://www-sul.stanford.edu/mac/parc.html.

Pang, Alex Soojung-Kim, and Wendy Marinaccio. "Making the Macintosh Home Page." *Making
the Macintosh: Technology and Culture in Silicon Valley*. http://www-sul.stanford.edu/mac
/index.html.

Patel, Nilay. "Jobs: If You See a Stylus or a Task Manager, 'They Blew It.'" *Engadget*, April 8, 2010. http://www.engadget.com/2010/04/08/jobs-if-you-see-a-stylus-or-a-task-manager-they -blew-it/.

"PDA Definition from PC Magazine Encyclopedia." http://www.pcmag.com/encyclopedia/term /49021/pda.

Periroth, Nicole. "For PrimeSense, Microsoft's Kinect Is Just the Beginning." *Forbes*, December 12, 2010. http://www.forbes.com/sites/nicoleperlroth/2010/12/13/for-primesense-microsofts -kinect-is-just-the-beginning/.

Pham, Alex. "E3: Microsoft Shows Off Gesture Control Technology for Xbox 360." *LA Times Blogs—Technology*, June 1, 2009. http://latimesblogs.latimes.com/technology/2009/06 /microsofte3.html.

"PLA (C64 Chip)." *C64-Wiki*, September 30, 2014. http://www.c64-wiki.com/index.php/PLA _(C64_chip).

Pogue, David. "Looking at the iPad from Two Angles." *New York Times*, March 31, 2010, sec. Technology / Personal Tech. http://www.nytimes.com/2010/04/01/technology /personaltech/01pogue.html.

Rao, Arun. "Early Failures: Good Ideas Which Arrive Early Are Bad Products (1980–94)." Excerpts from *A History of Silicon Valley* by Arun Rao and Piero Scaruffi, 2010. http://www.scaruffi .com/svhistory/sv/chap90.html.

Raskin, Jef. "Design Considerations for an Anthropophilic Computer." *Making the Macintosh: Technology and Culture in Silicon Valley*, May 29, 1979. http://www-sul.stanford.edu/mac /primary/docs/bom/anthrophilic.html.

———. "Down with GUIs!" *Wired*, December 1993. http://archive.wired.com/wired/archive /1.06/1.6_guis.html.

———. "General Criteria." In *The Macintosh Project: Selected Papers from Jef Raskin (First Macintosh Designer), circa 1979*, 1979. http://www-sul.stanford.edu/mac/primary/docs /bom/gencrit.html.

———. *The Humane Interface: New Directions for Designing Interactive Systems*. Reading, MA: Addison-Wesley, 2000.

Reimer, Jeremy. "From Altair to iPad: 35 Years of Personal Computer Market Share." *Ars Technica*, August 14, 2012. http://arstechnica.com/business/2012/08/from-altair-to-ipad-35-years-of -personal-computer-market-share/.

———. "Total Share: Personal Computer Market Share 1975–2010." *Jeremy's Blog*, December 7, 2012. http://jeremyreimer.com/m-item.lsp?i=137.

———. "Total Share: 30 Years of Personal Computer Market Share Figures." *Ars Technica*, December 15, 2005. http://arstechnica.com/features/2005/12/total-share/.

Rosenblatt, Roger. "A New World Dawns." *Time*, January 3, 1983. http://content.time.com/time /magazine/article/0,9171,953631,00.html.

Rutkowski, Chris. "An Introduction to the Human Applications Standard Computer Interface, Part 1: Theory and Principles." *Byte*, October 1982.

———. "An Introduction to the Human Applications Standard Computer Interface, Part 2: Implementing the HASCI Concept." *Byte*, November 1982. http://archive.org/details/byte-magazine-1982-11.

Sanford, Glen. "Graphical User Interface (GUI)." *Apple-History*, August 29, 2014. http://www.apple-history.com/gui.

———. "iPad." *Apple-History*, August 29, 2014. http://www.apple-history.com/ipad.

———. "Macintosh Plus." *Apple-History*, August 29, 2014. http://www.apple-history.com/plus.

Schembri, Thierry, and Olivier Boisseau. "Hewlett Packard HP-150." *OLD-COMPUTERS.COM*. http://www.old-computers.com/museum/computer.asp?st=1&c=139.

Scott, Ridley. *1984*. Apple, Inc., 1984.

Sculley, John. *Odyssey: Pepsi to Apple—A Journey of Adventure, Ideas, and the Future*. New York: Harper & Row, 1987.

"Sculley Clears Up Jobs 'Myths.'" *BBC News*. http://www.bbc.co.uk/news/technology-16538745.

Shklovsky, Viktor. "Art as Technique." In *Russian Formalist Criticism: Four Essays*, translated by Lee T. Lemon and Marion J. Reis, 3–24. Regents Critics Series. Lincoln: University of Nebraska Press, 1965.

Slade, Giles. *Made to Break: Technology and Obsolescence in America*. Cambridge, MA: Harvard University Press, 2006.

Smith, David Woodruff. *Husserl*. 2nd edition. London and New York: Routledge, 2013.

———. "Phenomenology." In *The Stanford Encyclopedia of Philosophy*, edited by Edward N. Zalta. Stanford, CA: The Metaphysics Research Lab, Center for the Study of Language and Information (CSLI), Stanford University, 2013. http://plato.stanford.edu/archives/win2013/entries/phenomenology/.

SRI International. *1968 Demo—FJCC Conference Presentation Reel #1*, 1968. http://archive.org/details/XD300–23_68HighlightsAResearchCntAugHumanIntellect.

———. *1968 Demo—FJCC Conference Presentation Reel #2*, 1968. http://archive.org/details/XD300–24_68HighlightsAResearchCntAugHumanIntellect.

———. *1968 Demo—FJCC Conference Presentation Reel #3*, 1968. http://archive.org/details/XD300–25_68HighlightsAResearchCntAugHumanIntellect.

Steil, Michael. "How Many Commodore 64 Computers Were Really Sold?" *Pagetable.com: Some Assembly Required*, February 1, 2011. http://www.pagetable.com/?p=547.

Stengel, Steven. "Apple II Computer." *Obsolete Technology Website*, March 1, 2014. http://oldcomputers.net/appleii.html.

———. "Apple Newton." *Obsolete Technology Website*, December 10, 2013. http://oldcomputers.net/apple-newton.html.

———. "AT&T EO 440 Personal Communicator." *Obsolete Technology Website*, May 19, 2014. http://oldcomputers.net/eo-440.html.

———. "Commodore 64 Computer." *Obsolete Technology Website*, July 21, 2014. http://oldcomputers.net/c64.html.

———. "Commodore Pet 2001 Computer." *Obsolete Technology Website*, December 10, 2013. http://oldcomputers.net/pet2001.html.

———. "GRiD Compass 1101 Computer." *Obsolete Technology Website*, April 20, 2014. http://oldcomputers.net/grid1101.html.

———. "GRiDPad." *Obsolete Technology Website*, December 10, 2013. http://oldcomputers.net/gridpad.html.

———. "IBM 5150 Personal Computer." *Obsolete Technology Website*, December 10, 2013. http://oldcomputers.net/ibm5150.html.

———. "Linus Write-Top Computer." *Obsolete Technology Website*, December 10, 2013. http://oldcomputers.net/linus.html.

———. "Tandy Radio Shack TRS-80 Model I Computer." *Obsolete Technology Website*, December 10, 2013. http://oldcomputers.net/trs80i.html.

Stephenson, Neal. "In the Beginning . . .Was the Command Line," 1999. http://pauillac.inria.fr/~weis/info/commandline.html.

Steve Jobs and Bill Gates Together in 2007 at D5, 2012. http://www.youtube.com/watch?v=ZWaX1g_2SSQ&feature=youtube_gdata_player.

Steve Jobs Introduces Original iPad—Apple Special Event (2010), 2013. http://www.youtube.com/watch?v=_KN-5zmvjAo.

Steve Jobs Introduces the Original Macintosh—Apple Shareholder Event (1984), 2013. http://www.youtube.com/watch?v=YShLWK9n2Sk&feature=youtube_gdata_player.

Steve Jobs iPhone 2007 Presentation (Full HD), 2013. http://www.youtube.com/watch?v=vN4U5FqrOdQ&feature=youtube_gdata_player.

Steve Jobs on the Post PC Era, 2013. http://www.youtube.com/watch?v=YfJ3QxJYsw8&feature=youtube_gdata_player.

Steve Jobs: "Who Wants a Stylus?"—Apple—Steve Jobs at Macworld 2007 in San Francisco, 2010. http://www.youtube.com/watch?v=4YY3MSaUqMg&feature=youtube_gdata_player.

Streeter, Thomas. *The Net Effect: Romanticism, Capitalism, and the Internet*. Critical Cultural Communication. New York: New York University Press, 2011.

Suggett, Paul. "Profile of TBWA/Chiat/Day." *About.com*. http://advertising.about.com/od/unitedstates/a/Tbwa-Chiat-Day.htm.

Thomson, James. "Continuity of States in Matter." In *Collected Papers in Physics and Engineering*, edited by Joseph Larmor and James C. Thomson, 276–333. Cambridge: Cambridge University Press, 1912. http://archive.org/details/collectedpapersi00thomrich.

"TIME Magazine Cover: The Computer, Machine of the Year—Jan. 3, 1983." *TIME.com*. http://content.time.com/time/covers/0,16641,19830103,00.html.

Topolsky, Joshua. "Apple iPad Review." *Engadget*, April 3, 2010. http://www.engadget.com
/2010/04/03/apple-ipad-review/.

Tracy, Ed. "History of Computer Design: Apple Macintosh." *Apple and the History of Personal
Computer Design*. http://www.landsnail.com/apple/local/design/macintosh.html.

———. "History of Computer Design: Commodore VIC-20 & 64." *Apple and the History of Personal
Computer Design*. http://www.landsnail.com/apple/local/design/commodore.html.

———. "History of Computer Design: Macintosh Plus." *Apple and the History of Personal
Computer Design*. http://www.landsnail.com/apple/local/design/macplus.html.

Tuan, Yi-Fu. *Space and Place: The Perspective of Experience*. Minneapolis: University of Minnesota
Press, 1977.

Turkle, Sherry. *The Second Self: Computers and the Human Spirit*. 20th anniversary ed. Cambridge,
MA: MIT Press, 2005.

Veit, Stan. "The Commodore 64." *PC History.org*. http://www.pc-history.org/comm.htm.

Wardrip-Fruin, Noah, and Nick Montfort, eds. *The NewMediaReader*. Cambridge, MA: MIT Press,
2003.

Weiser, Mark. "The Computer for the 21st Century." *Scientific American* 265, no. 3 (September
1991): 91–94. doi:10.1038/scientificamerican0991-94.

Weyhrich, Steven. *Sophistication & Simplicity: The Life and Times of the Apple II Computer*.
Winnipeg, MB: Variant Press, 2013.

Wiener, Norbert. *Cybernetics*. New York: J. Wiley, 1948.

———. *The Human Use of Human Beings: Cybernetics and Society*. Da Capo Series in Science.
New York: Da Capo Press, 1988.

———. "Men, Machines, and the World About." In *The NewMediaReader*, edited by Noah Wardrip-
Fruin and Nick Montfort, 67–72. Cambridge, MA: MIT Press, 2003.

Italicized page numbers indicate illustrations.